LOND
CAFÉS, COFFEE
SHOPS & TEAROOMS

David Hampshire

Survival Books • Bath • England

First published 2016

Survival Books Limited
Office 169, 3 Edgar Buildings
George Street, Bath BA1 2FJ, United Kingdom
+44 (0)1225-462135, info@survivalbooks.net
www.survivalbooks.net and www.londons-secrets.com

British Library Cataloguing in Publication Data
A CIP record for this book is available
from the British Library.

ISBN: 978-1-909282-80-3

Printed in China

Acknowledgements

The author would like to thank all those who helped with research and provided information for this book, particularly Graeme & Louise Chesters, Robert Johnston, Joanna and Michael Mitchell, and many others – who are unfortunately too numerous to mention here. Special thanks are also due to Robbi Atilgan for editing; Peter Read for additional editing and proof-reading; David Woodworth for final proof checking; John Marshall for DTP, photo selection and cover design; Jim Watson for his expert advice on layout and design, and the author's partner for the constant supply of tea, coffee, food and wine (and for continuing with the pretence that writing is a real job).

Last, but not least, a special thank you to the many photographers – the unsung heroes – whose beautiful images bring London to life.

The Author

David Hampshire's career has taken him around the world and he lived and worked in many countries before taking up writing full-time in the '80s. He's the author, co-author or editor of some 25 titles, including *London for Foodies, Gourmets & Gluttons, London's Secret Places, London's Secrets: Museums & Galleries, London's Secrets: Parks & Gardens, London's Secrets: Peaceful Places* and *A Year in London*. David was born in Surrey but lived and worked in London for many years and still considers himself a Londoner. He now divides his time between London and Bath.

Readers' Guide

♦ **Contact details:** These include the address, telephone number and website (where applicable). You can enter the postcode to display a map of the location on Google Maps and other map sites or put the postcode into a satnav. The nearest tube or railway station, as applicable, is also listed.

♦ **Opening hours:** These can change at short notice, so you should confirm times by telephone or check the website before travelling. Some venues close on one or two days a week, which is indicated, and some are closed at weekends, e.g. in the City.

♦ **Prices:** We have not indicated prices for cafés, coffee shops and tearooms, all of which are usually reasonable (some are a bargain) and generally vary little. The exceptions are breakfast/brunch, which although good value in most places can be relatively expensive in upmarket venues, and afternoon tea, where we have included a guide price (some venues are eye-wateringly expensive).

♦ **Bookings:** Most places listed in this book can be visited spontaneously, although some require bookings for lunch and/or brunch. You generally always need to book for lunch or brunch in a restaurant or hotel, and bookings are almost always required for afternoon tea whatever the venue (some also have dress codes). Note, however, that some restaurants don't accept bookings and you just have to turn up and join the queue.

Café, Coffee Shop or Tearoom?

There is often very little obvious difference between cafés, coffee shops and tearooms, and many establishments manage to be a combination of all three; all do breakfast and many also offer brunch, and – not surprisingly – tearooms also serve afternoon tea. We have endeavoured to categorise venues according to their speciality, although many could have been included in a number of chapters.

Contents

Introduction

This book is a celebration of London's ever-increasing wealth of excellent independent cafés, coffee shops and tearooms – as well as places specialising in afternoon tea, breakfast and brunch – all of which have enjoyed a renaissance in the last decade and done much to strengthen the city's position as one of the world's leading foodie destinations.

The number and variety of independent cafés in London has flourished in recent years, and if the city didn't have a café culture a few decades ago, it certainly does now. The quality and variety of food and drink served in cafés has improved beyond recognition in the past ten years, and is now on a par with (or better) than that of many restaurants – and the bill is invariably much lower. In fact, if you want to have a good lunch (or, increasingly, dinner) in London and don't want to pay a fortune, a café is often your best bet.

Coffee sales in Britain have grown rapidly in the last decade or so, as has the number of coffee shops, importers and roasteries that have sprung up around the capital. London's love affair with the bean has gone, quite literally, from strength to strength; not so many years ago it was difficult to find anything but insipid, luke-warm coffee, but now fresh bean-powered brews are everywhere, thanks in no small part to a host of expat baristas and coffee roasters from Down Under.

The British are famous for their love of a good cup of tea – which, as every native knows, cures all ills – although nowadays it's just as likely to be a delicate white, energising green, aromatic and complex oolong or a mysterious aged pu'er, as it is good ol' builder's brew. London has an abundance of specialist tearooms, many with expert 'tearistas' (tea baristas) on hand to proffer advice, where you can enjoy fine teas in a delightful setting.

Tea is also a vital component of the quintessentially English diversion of afternoon tea. London's leading hotels – along with hundreds of restaurants, cafés and tearooms – compete to produce the most lavish and original afternoon tea, consisting of exquisite teas, divine cakes, pastries and savouries – and even cocktails and champagne!

If there's one meal that the British can claim their own, it's the cooked breakfast. This world-famous indulgence traditionally takes the form of a huge fry-up – the 'full English' – but in today's foodie London it's

just as likely to include a wealth of tasty and original dishes with influences from around the globe. Increasingly, it has competition from its stay-a-bed cousin, brunch – a moreish marriage of breakfast and lunch – which Londoners have taken to with a passion in recent years.

With a copy of *London's Cafés, Coffee Shops & Tearooms* – featuring over 250 venues – you'll never be lost for somewhere to treat yourself to a great cup of coffee, a pot of exquisite tea or a plate of delicious food. We hope you enjoy discovering the city's burgeoning café culture as much as we did.

David Hampshire
January 2016

1. Cafés

The growth of London's independent café scene over the last ten years or so has done much to reinforce the city's position as one of the world's gastronomic capitals. These days, it seems that there are cafés on every corner: no-frills traditional 'caffs' – known affectionately as 'greasy spoons' – serving honest British grub such as the full English breakfast; homely, characterful neighbourhood cafés specialising in high-quality drinks and homemade food; new wave rustic cafés serving artisan brews, with inventive menus (and wine lists) befitting a quality restaurant; and chic designer cafés that wouldn't be out of place in Paris or Rome.

This chapter features 90 of London's best independent cafés, chosen primarily for the excellence of their beverages, particularly their coffee and tea, and tasty food, which is usually made in-house. However, friendly staff, efficient service, appealing décor, free wifi, good value, a pleasing ambience and a great location all play their part in creating a must-visit café.

London may not have the abundant pavement cafés of continental Europe – or the sunshine in which to enjoy them – but it has created its own unique brand of café culture with something for everyone: traditional or contemporary, continental or Antipodean, unpretentious or sophisticated.

202 Café

This popular, elegant café, secreted away in an up-market Nicole Farhi boutique in Westbourne Grove, has simple yet classic décor, with aged wood, vintage touches and monochrome fashions. During the week it's a peaceful place to enjoy excellent morning coffee, while at weekends you're likely to have to queue for a table (there's also a small terrace, but you need to arrive early to bag a spot there).

202 serves great breakfast/brunch classics and dinner (Fri-Sat) featuring brasserie-inspired dishes at around the £13-£15 mark, such as spinach, pumpkin and ricotta lasagne, lamb burger with goat's cheese, and marinated swordfish steak with saffron and orzo salad.

202 Café, 202 Westbourne Grove, W11 2SB (020-7727 2722; www.202london.com; Notting Hill Gate tube; Mon 10am-6pm, Tue-Thu 8.30am-6pm, Fri-Sat 8.30am-10pm, Sun 10am-5pm).

Albion

One of Shoreditch's hidden gems, the Conran-owned Albion is a posh café and small deli, with an in-house bakery and cake counter. It's located within the stylish Boundary building, seating 60 inside and a further 30 outside.

The all-day breakfast menu includes a hearty 'full English', a variety of treats on toast – from bacon and kidneys to fried duck eggs – omelettes and eggs in any style, even kippers if you will. The accompanying all-day menu offers Welsh rarebit, ham and mustard sandwich, devilled kidneys, mackerel salad, sausage and mash, and fish and chips. There's also a market shop selling fresh bread, cakes, and fruit and veg.

Albion, 2-4 Boundary St, E2 7DD (020-7729 1051; http://albioncaff.co.uk; Shoreditch High St rail; Sun-Wed 8am-11pm, Thu-Sat 8am-1am).

Andersen & Co

In recent years Del Boy's manor of Peckham has gone from strength to strength, particularly the increasingly posh Bellenden Road, where a plethora of trendy cafés and eating places have sprung up. One of these is Andersen & Co, a licensed, family-run, café-brasserie established in 2010 and now a firm neighbourhood favourite. With a lovely bright (white and pale grey) interior and a delightful rear courtyard garden filled with plants and flowers, it's a lovely spot to spend some time.

Serving Square Mile coffee, Birchall teas and a wide range of Brick House and Blackbird Bakery breads, Andersen has an extensive breakfast/lunch menu (served until 3pm), a weekend brunch menu (9am-3pm) and Sunday lunch (12.30-3pm). It also offers a selection of homemade cakes and pastries

(try the courgette cake with crème fraîche and lemon curd), award-winning sandwiches, salads and lunch specials.

Dinner is served from Thursday to Saturday, when you can enjoy (among other things – see website) tasty Peckham burgers, panko and parmesan crumbed chicken breast, bavette steak and frites, pan fried cod, salted caramel banoffee pie, brownie and vanilla ice cream parfait, and local craft beers. Super!

Anderson & Co, 139 Bellenden Rd, SE15 4DH (020-7469 7078; www.andersonandcompany. co.uk; Peckham Rye rail; Mon-Wed 8am-5pm, Thu-Sat 8am-10.30pm, Sun 8.30am-4.30pm).

Arlo & Moe

Run by a brother and sister-in law team, Arlo & Moe is a friendly, laid-back neighbourhood café occupying a former barber shop. A firm family favourite, well-stocked with highchairs and baby-changing facilities, A&M has a retro '50s vibe with colourful Formica tables, Ercol chairs and quirky posters on the walls.

A&M serve excellent Dark Fluid coffee, imaginative lunchtime fare, and an irresistible selection of cakes and sweet treats (try the chocolate and Guinness cake). They offer a wider than average range of brunch options, including sausage rolls, sandwiches, frittata, quiche, soup of the day and specials. Try the invitingly-named 'sexy toast' – crunchy sourdough topped with cream cheese and honey, avocado and feta or homely baked beans.

Arlo & Moe, 340 Brockley Rd, SE4 2BT (07749-667207; Crofton Pak rail; Mon-Fri 8am-4.30pm, Sat 9am-4pm, Sun 10am-4pm).

Barmouth Kitchen

This small independent community café in Wandsworth is a genuine local concern, run by ten families with neighbourhood roots who know what their customers want. Barmouth Kitchen serves food and drink in a welcoming, friendly atmosphere, including excellent coffee (Union) and tea (Teapigs). Much of the food is sourced from local suppliers or made in-house, including a range of artisan breads, cakes and pastries.

Barmouth serves robust breakfasts, spoil-yourself weekend brunches, tasty lunches (including kids' meals to eat in or take away), as well as a range of home-cooked,

take-away frozen meals, so that you can have a 'proper' meal without having to cook it. The café is also licensed.

Barmouth Kitchen, 2 Barmouth Rd, SW18 2DN (020-8704 4413; www.barmouthkitchen. co.uk; Wandsworth Town rail; Mon-Sat 8.30am-5.30pm, Sun 9am-1pm).

Birdie Num Nums

Established in 2013 by sisters Sevjan Melissa and Akjen Havali, Birdie Num Nums (from Peter Sellers '60s comedy film, *The Party*) is a delightful little café in New Cross. Along with the usual full English, scrambled eggs and BLTs, it serves Turkish treats with a modern twist, including a 'full Turkish' breakfast, chargrilled halloumi bruschetta and irresistible baklava, alongside more unusual flavours such as dark chocolate-infused Quorn chilli nachos. Drinks include coffee from Hackney-based Climpson, tea from local company Birchall, plus Firefly tonics, delicious hot chocolate and homemade limonata.

As if that wasn't enough, there's also live music, comedy, saucy belly dancing and cheeky burlesque nights (with a pop-up bar). What's not to like?

Birdie Num Nums, 11 Lewisham Way, SE14 6PP (020-8692 7223; http://birdienumnums. co.uk; New Cross rail; Tue-Sat 9am-6pm, Sun 9am-5pm).

Blue Brick Café

A former Victorian dairy, the charming Blue Brick Café was reincarnated in 2010 by Daniel Hughes as a vegetarian café/bistro. The blue-tiled café has a homely interior furnished with old wooden tables and school chairs, and decorated with old bottles and vases filled with flowers.

All-day breakfast ranges from muesli to a full vegetarian English with sourdough toast. Using fresh local produce, Dan produces simple, rustic dishes, including soups and salads (try the goat's cheese with roasted peppers and Puy lentils) and tasty mains such as spring vegetable risotto and spicy chickpea stew. There are also proper desserts like spiced apple and plum crumble. Everything is fresh, delicious and terrific value.

Blue Brick Café, 14 Fellbrigg Rd, SE22 9HH (020-8299 8670; www.bluebrickcafe.com; E Dulwich rail; Mon-Sat 9am-5.30pm, Sun 9.30am-5pm).

Bluebelles

A beautiful café at the northern end of Portobello Road, Bluebelles is a great place to fuel up before seeking bargains in the nearby market. This rustic, homely, vintage-styled café – with its cool, shabby-chic décor and a few outside tables – is just perfect for a relaxing breakfast, brunch or light lunch.

The inviting window display heaves with home-baked (in-house) diet-busting delights – try the white chocolate, raspberry and cardamom cake – while inside there's a selection of delicious pastries, croissants (the almond ones are scrummy), tasty sandwiches, salads and soups, plus a wealth of savoury delights, such as eggs Benedict and bacon sarnies. The excellent coffee is from Caravan.

Bluebelles, 320 Portobello Rd, W10 5RU (020-8968 4572; Ladbroke Grove tube; Mon-Fri 8am-5pm, Sat-Sun 9am-5pm).

The Brew House Café

Tucked away in beautiful landscaped parkland on Hampstead Heath, the Brew House Café (managed by Searcys) is located in Grade II* listed Kenwood House, one of the most magnificent estates in London. Although there's ample seating inside this is primarily an alfresco venue, with umbrella-shaded tables spread across the delightful sheltered terrace.

There's a reasonably comprehensive breakfast menu, including a full English, while lunchtime offers a choice of hot and cold dishes. Drinks, sandwiches, cakes and pastries are served all day – and you can also enjoy (champagne) afternoon tea.

The Brew House Café, Kenwood House, Hampstead Ln, NW3 7JR (020-8348 4073; http:// searcys.co.uk/venues/kenwood-house/eat-drink; Archway or Golders Grn tube; daily 9am to 4 or 6pm, depending on the season).

Bygga Bo

Bygga Bo (meaning 'to make a nest' in Swedish) is a real find in not-so trendy Walthamstow – a cosy Swedish café with a lovely decked courtyard garden. The décor is a comfortable mix of vintage and contemporary, with a jumble of old chairs and tables, original mirrors, brass-panelled ceiling and hair-perming heaters converted into lights.

The excellent coffee is from Climpson, served with soya or almond milk at no extra cost, while all food is made in-house using traditional recipes and organic ingredients. For breakfast you can tuck into ever-popular cinnamon buns or quinoa porridge topped with pomegranate, while lunch offers open or toasted sandwiches topped with prawns, blue cheese or addictive Swedish meatballs.

Bygga Bo, 8 Chingford Rd, E17 4PJ (020-8527 3652; www.byggabo.com; Walthamstow Central tube; Mon, Wed-Fri 9am-5pm, Sat-Sun 9am-6pm, closed Tue).

Café in the Crypt

St Martin's Café in the Crypt – *Les Routiers* Café of the Year 2012 – is a enchanting place to have a drink or meal in central London. The crypt's beautiful 18th-century architecture (with brick-vaulted ceilings) is a feast for your eyes, while the tantalising menu ensures that your stomach isn't left out. The home-cooked food is freshly prepared on-site using ingredients from sustainable sources (where

possible) and is good value; a full English breakfast costs just £7.50 and Sunday roast (lunch) is a snip at just £9.95.

Open seven days a week for breakfast through to dinner (closes 6pm on Sundays), with live jazz on Wednesday evenings.

Café in the Crypt, St Martin-in-the-Fields, Trafalgar Sq, WC2N 4JJ (020-7766 1158; www. stmartin-in-the-fields.org/cafe-in-the-crypt; Charing Cross/Leicester Sq tube; Mon-Tue 8am-8pm, Wed 8am-10.30pm, Thu-Sat 8am-9pm, Sun 11am-6pm).

Café Laville

An Italian café bridging the canal in picturesque Little Venice, Café Laville is a lovely spot in which to enjoy everything from continental breakfast (try yogurt with honey and almonds or omelette with goat's cheese and spinach), a freshly-made sandwich or salad at lunch, or a tasty dinner of pasta, risotto or grilled fish/meat. The rustic and contemporary Italian Mediterranean food is delicious and accompanied by a selection of Italian wines.

On sunny days there are few better places to enjoy a coffee or hearty breakfast/brunch than the café's terrace overlooking the tranquil Grand Union canal. Bliss.

Café Laville, 453 Edgware Rd, W2 1HT (020-7706 2620; www.cafelaville.co.uk; Paddington tube/rail; daily 10am-10pm).

Café Moka

Owned by Mauritian cook Kevin Vanthem, Moka (named after a town in Mauritius) is a light and airy friendly neighbourhood café close to Harringay railway station, just north of Finsbury Park. The warm and rustic interior – exposed brick and lots of wood – vintage furniture, book shelves, open-plan kitchen and a tranquil walled courtyard out back (blankets are provided for inclement days) make for a homely atmosphere.

Moka offers good coffee, excellent tea (Teapigs) and luscious homemade cakes, including fantastic chocolate brownies, coffee and walnut cake and muffins. The café does lovely breakfasts and lunches too, and also sells bread from a local artisan baker to take home. Great value!

Café Moka, 5 Wightman Rd, N4 1RQ (020-8340 8664; Harringay rail; Mon-Fri 8am-5pm, Sat 9am-5pm, Sun 9am-4pm).

Café Riva

A fixture on Borough High Street since 1966, Café Riva is certainly no greasy spoon; restyled in 2012, it occupies a spacious bright room with a huge counter bursting with scrumptious homemade food. Not surprisingly for a place that caters for Borough Market visitors and opens at 6am, Riva specialises in breakfasts, offering everything from porridge and granola to a filling farmer's English breakfast, accompanied by excellent Monmouth coffee and quality teas.

All food is prepared to order (made with market-fresh ingredients) and includes delicious ciabatta melts, tasty pasta dishes, jacket potatoes and a choice of daily specials. Friendly staff, reasonable prices and appetising food – a winner!

Café Riva, 200 Borough High St, SE1 1JX (020-7407 0737; www.caferiva.co.uk; Borough tube; Mon-Fri 6am-4pm, Sat 8am-3pm, Sun 8am-2.30pm).

Chelsea Quarter Café

Located around ten minutes' walk from Sloane Square, the stylish licensed Chelsea Quarter Café is part of a small chain (see website). The charming CQC occupies a large corner site in this tranquil part of Chelsea, with an enticing window display of cakes and pastries concealing a large elegant interior.

The menu includes wholesome all-day breakfasts (try the delicious eggs Benedict), light lunches – homemade soups, dips and salads, sandwiches (try the moreish avocado and buffalo mozzarella baguette with sun-dried tomato and pesto), pasta dishes, plus 'chef's favourites' – as well as freshly-baked pastries, cakes and tarts. Drinks include excellent coffee and teas, fresh fruit juices and some of the best smoothies in town.

Chelsea Quarter Café, 219 King's Rd, SW3 5EJ (020-7352 3660; www.chelseaquartercafe.com; Sloane Sq tube; Mon-Sat 7.30am-8pm, Sun 8am-7pm).

Chinwag

Chinwag is an eccentric café/bistro in New Cross (opposite Goldsmiths Uni) serving good coffee and delicious burgers. You enter through an red phone box door, while inside there's exposed brickwork, a hodgepodge of old tables (including school desks), flowers in buckets, wall lights created from taps, bicycle wheel 'chandeliers' and a lovely vintage cash register. There's also a decked area out front for sunny days.

Chinwag specialises in big breakfasts (eggs, crispy hash browns, ham, sausages and fried tomatoes, although for the health conscious there are also granola, porridge, yoghurt, berries, etc.) and even bigger gourmet hamburgers (beef, lamb, chicken or veggie) served with aioli, lettuce, tomato and relish in light sesame buns – delicious! Alcohol licence, reasonable prices, friendly staff and cool tunes = café heaven.

Chinwag, 21 Lewisham Way, SE14 6PP (New Cross rail; Mon-Sat 10am-10pm, Sun 10am-5pm).

The Clerkenwell Kitchen

Serving breakfast, lunch and afternoon tea, the Clerkenwell Kitchen is a bright and airy café with a spacious courtyard terrace (but only six tables and no bookings), catering to the smart young Clerkenwell set. The exposed architectural features, white walls and industrial open kitchen are complemented by wooden floors, culinary-themed line drawings and a wood burner.

The Kitchen sources most of its produce locally and specialises in seasonal, sustainable, organic and free-range food. The changing lunch menu includes six daily specials and puddings and a choice of freshly-made sourdough sandwiches, tarts and soups, plus tempting home-baked cakes. It's also licensed and serves Fairtrade teas and coffees and organic fruit juices.

The Clerkenwell Kitchen, 27-31 Clerkenwell Close, EC1R 0AT (020-7101 9959; www. theclerkenwellkitchen.co.uk; Farringdon rail/ Barbican tube; Mon-Fri 8am-5pm, closed weekends).

The Cloister Café

Located in the beautiful 15th-century cloisters of Great St Bartholomew's church, this is one of London's loveliest and most tranquil cafés. Usually open daily (except Saturday, but check) the Cloister serves excellent coffee, tea (including fresh mint tea), soft drinks, cider, house wines and (appropriately) monastic beers. There's also a selection of cakes and pastries, homemade quiche, tasty pies, cheese platters, charcuterie, hearty stews and soup. Heavenly fare indeed!

There's a fee of £4 to visit St Barts – London's oldest church and well worth a tour – but access to the café is free.

Cloister Café, St Bartholomew the Great, W Smithfield, EC1A 9DS (020-7600 0440; www. greatstbarts.com/pages/cloister_cafe/cafe. html; Barbican tube; Mon-Fri 8.30am-5pm (4pm from mid-Nov to mid-Feb), Sun 9.30am-6.30pm, closed Sat).

Cooper & Wolf

A family run café-restaurant in Clapton overlooking Millfields Park, Cooper & Wolf (named after the owners' cats) occupies a lovely, bright corner building (a former glazer's shop) with huge picture windows.

The café is run by friendly Swede Sara and specialises in home-cooked Swedish dishes such as meatballs, *gravlax* (cured salmon) and *inlagd sill* (pickled herring), plus a range of vegetarian options.

C&W also serve excellent coffee (Caravan) and tea (Make Tea Not War) and soft drinks, and bake their own delicious cinnamon buns (*kanelbullar*) and a selection of cakes daily. A friendly, homespun delight.

Cooper & Wolf, 145 Chatsworth Rd, E5 0LA (www.cooperandwolf.co.uk; Clapton rail; Mon-Thu 9am-5.30pm, Fri 9am-6pm, Sat-Sun 10am-6pm).

Cornerstone Café

Occupying an old warehouse (formerly part of a munitions factory) at Royal Arsenal Riverside, the Cornerstone Café must be one of the largest neighbourhood cafés in London. It's a beautifully designed, relaxing and sympathetic space which retains much of its original character while at the same time being very modern and chic, with bespoke oak tables, banquette seating, white chairs and light fittings, and a glass roof that floods the room with light.

Cornerstone offers comprehensive breakfast and brunch (weekends only) menus until 3pm including all the usual favourites, plus a wide range of cakes and pastries, excellent coffee (Union) and a wide choice of loose-leaf teas. For lunch there's a large selection of sandwiches, soups, salads and tasty hot meals, including fishcakes, homemade pies, tortilla, roast chicken, salmon, and mushroom and rosemary tagliatelle.

There's also a corner dedicated to take-home treats such as gourmet sauces, chutneys, oils, vinegars and – for those who have no time to cook – a daily take-away dinner.

Cornerstone Café, 9 Major Draper St, SE18 6GD (020-8316 4361; www.thecornerstonecafe. co.uk; Woolwich Arsenal DLR/rail; Mon-Fri 7am-8pm, Sat-Sun 9.30am-5pm).

La Cuisine de Bar

This chic café shares its address with the Chelsea branch of Poilâne *boulangerie* and is a French classic, serving a variety of sweet and savoury pastries in a bright and airy space filled with the intoxicating aroma of freshly-baked bread.

Good-value bread baskets with various spreads are popular, as are the range of *tartines* – toasted open sandwiches – prepared to order in front of you. For those with a sweet tooth there's a variety of Viennoiserie, gingerbread, buttery *punition* cookies and more. *Délicieux!*

Cuisine de Bar, 39 Cadogan Gdns, SW3 2TB (020-3263 6019; www.cuisinedebar.fr/en; Sloane Sq tube; Mon-Fri 8am-8.30pm, Sat-Sun 9am-6.30pm).

Curious Yellow Kafé

This cool, stylish café serves Swedish and British dishes – including a weekend Scandi breakfast with *gravlax*, ham, cheese, pâté, gherkins and crudités, served with a selection of Swedish breads. The small IKEA-esque interior has a cosy and inviting atmosphere, while outside there's plenty of seating under bright yellow parasols (matching the startling yellow door).

The Kafé offers a range of breakfast, brunch and lunch options, including excellent coffee and Swedish teas (Johan & Nyström), tasty pastries and tarts, egg-based dishes, sweet and savoury croissants, sandwiches and salads, plus heartier fare such as curries, stews, pies and more. *Smaklig målted!*

Curious Yellow Kafé, 77 Pitfield St, N1 6BT (020-7251 6018; Hoxton/Old St rail; Mon-Wed 8am-6pm, Thu-Fri 8am-7pm, Sat-Sun 9am-7pm).

Daisy Green

Daisy Green is the brainchild of Aussie-born Prue Freeman, who is passionate about bold, healthy, fresh (organic if possible) food, most of which is made in-house using locally-sourced seasonal produce. Sitting on the corner of Portman Village, a few streets from Marble Arch, it's an attractive, stylish café (over two floors) with a large picture window, faux green grass, neon-coloured deckchairs and DAISY in lights above the door (it's much more attractive than it sounds).

Daisy offers excellent coffee (they even roast their own beans) and tea, juices and smoothies, homemade cakes (delicious banana cake, moreish chocolate brownies, etc.), gourmet frozen yogurt (the house speciality), and tasty salads and wraps that change daily. Bonzer!

Daisy Green, 20 Seymour St, W1H 7HX (020-7723 3301; www.daisygreenfood.com; Marble Arch tube; Mon-Fri 7am-5.30pm, Sat-Sun 9am-5.30pm).

Daylesford Organic

The pioneers and undisputed kings of organic farming, Daylesford established its first London base at this Pimlico address, hosting a farm shop and café. The large, well-designed shop, with clean white spaces and grey marble, offers three floors of top quality organic food to eat in or take home.

The vast upstairs café serves mostly Daylesford's own produce; everything is organic and/or sustainably sourced – and delicious, too. The vast menu includes breakfast, weekend brunch, lunch and afternoon tea – there's even a supper club. Not the cosiest or cheapest café in town (it's Pimlico after all), but a superb spot for a healthy breakfast or lunch.

Daylesford Farmshop & Café, 44B Pimlico Rd, SW1W 8LP (020-7881 8060; http://daylesford. com/pimlico; Sloane Sq tube; Mon-Sat 8am-6pm, Sun 10am-3pm).

The De Beauvoir Deli Co.

De Beauvoir is a café/deli in Islington opened in 2009 by Harry Davies, which has flourished ever since. It attracts a loyal band of foodies who love their locally-sourced products, including organic fruit and veg, artisan cheeses and healthy ready meals prepared in-house.

At one end of the shop there are tables and chairs where you can tuck into a wholesome breakfast – the all-day cooked breakfast comes in two sizes – or enjoy a pot of granola with compote or honey, bagels, croissants, toast and more. There's also good coffee along with a selection of homemade pastries and cakes, and a huge choice of delicious sandwiches and tasty meat platters for lunch.

The De Beauvoir Deli Co, 98 Southgate Rd, N1 3JD (020-7249 4321; http://thedebeauvoirdeli. co.uk; Essex Rd/Haggerston rail; Mon-Fri 8am-8pm, Sat 8am-6pm, Sun 9am-4pm).

Drawing Room Café

A lovely café secreted away in Fulham Place alongside the Thames in west London, the Drawing Room is a welcoming retreat – a rather grand sitting room with comfy sofas and armchairs and free newspapers. The licensed café offers a variety of indulgent cakes and pastries, hot and cold drinks, plus a light breakfast menu during the week (full English at weekends from 9.30am-noon) and afternoon tea.

There's also a seasonal lunch menu, including a choice of light hot meals, soups, sandwiches, toasties and ice-cream. In summer the French doors open out onto a beautiful outdoor terrace (overlooking the gardens), where you can enjoy barbecued food and a jug of Pimm's. Delightful!

Drawing Room Café, Fulham Palace, Bishop's Ave, SW6 6EA (020-7736 3233; www. fulhampalace.org/visiting/drawing-room-cafe; Putney Br tube; daily 9.30am-4pm or 5pm).

Dreyfus Café

Dreyfus is an independent neighbourhood café and cake bakery overlooking Clapton Square in the historic heart of Hackney. Serving first-rate coffee (Has Bean) and tea, it's another Scandi-inspired café offering a range of northern European (and American) delights such as cinnamon buns, Nordic meatballs and mash with beetroot/lingonberry sauce, and chicken and dill crepes with sour cream.

Dreyfus is noted for its superb breakfast/brunch which includes eggs every which way (Benedict, Florentine, etc.) with muffins, Bircher muesli, pancakes, croissants, bacon buns, and scrambled egg and smoked salmon, in addition to a hearty full English. There's also a wide range of homemade cakes, pastries, sandwiches, lunch dishes and award-winning ice-cream, sorbets and milkshakes.

Dreyfus Café, 19 Lower Clapton Rd, E5 0NS (020-8985 4311; www.dreyfuscafe.co.uk; Hackney Central rail; Mon-Fri 8am-6pm, Sat-Sun 9am-5pm).

Esters

Esters is a friendly little neighbourhood café – previously Fred & Fran's – in Stoke Newington serving delicious coffee (Has Bean), tea (Postcard) and juices (Hill Farm, Hampshire), along with croissants from Yeast Bakery, and Eccles cakes and doughnuts from St John Bakery. However, it isn't all bought-in – homemade tidbits include almond milk, lemonade, granola, jams, pickles, relishes, cakes and pastries.

Breakfast offerings comprise the usual suspects – sourdough toast, Bircher muesli, French toast, eggs various ways

– while brunch/lunch features a seasonal hot food menu including dishes such as Jersey Royals, radish and goat's cheese, and grilled asparagus, yoghurt and poached egg. Scrummy!

Esters, 55 Kynaston Rd, N16 0EB (020-7254 0253; www.estersn16.com; Stoke Newington rail; Tue-Sat 9am-5pm, Sun 10am-4pm, closed Mon).

Fernandez & Wells

Fernandez & Wells started life in 2007 in Soho's Lexington Street and now boasts six outlets (see website), of which this is the largest and grandest. It occupies three impressive rooms in the east wing of 18th-century Somerset House, where Jorge Fernandez and Rick Wells have transported

their signature Spanish 'street-style' café into a lovely light space with views over the fountain courtyard. The décor incorporates York stone, wood and metal; oversized geometric paintings by British artist David Tremlett decorate the walls, while a long, cool bar bisects the main café area.

Spain dominates the F&W menu, which revolves around coffee, cured meats, cheese and wine, and takes in breakfast, lunch and dinner. There's a wide choice of tasty tapas, inventive sandwiches (try the aubergine, goat's cheese and pesto in a brioche bun) and splendid soups such as classic gazpacho. The 'ham room', where plump hams hang from the wall, dispenses slices of

lomito ibérico and *jamón de lampiño* – ham to die for!

There's also a range of enticing homemade cakes and pastries, including old-fashioned Eccles cakes. Excellent service and lip-smacking, value-for-money food. *Fantástico!*

Fernandez & Wells, Somerset House, Strand, WC2R 1LA (020-7420 9408; www. fernandezandwells.com; Temple tube; Mon-Fri 8am-11pm, Sat 10am-10pm, Sun 10am-8pm).

Fleet River Bakery

Part of London's new wave of innovative cafés, the Fleet River Bakery occupies a smart corner building with high arched windows and a few alfresco tables. Inside it's welcoming and homely, with a large seating area decorated with reclaimed wood and vintage furniture (and free wifi).

This licensed café is a beacon of hospitality, offering excellent coffee (Monmouth), iced lattes and a range of fancy teas, plus tasty sandwiches and baked treats – try the croissants stuffed with tomato and brie – and scrumptious cakes. Thursday and Friday are wine and cheese nights.

Fleet River Bakery, 71 Lincoln's Inn Fields, WC2A 3JF (020-7691 1457; www. fleetriverbakery.com; Holborn tube; Mon-Wed 7am-7pm, Thu-Fri 7am-9pm, Sat 9am-6pm, Sun 9.30am-5pm).

Fowlds Café

Fowlds café opened in 2014 at the front of Fowlds upholstery workshop (London's oldest upholsterers, est. 1870) in Camberwell. It's unusual as it's a joint collaboration between Bob Fowlds and the residents of Addington Square, who fill the café with flowers, art works and the usual café sundries, while retaining the workshop vibe.

During the day Fowlds serves excellent coffee (Square Mile), cakes, pastries, sandwiches and home-cooked meals from a seasonal daily-changing menu, while on Thu-Fri evenings it morphs into a bar serving rustic bar snacks (cheese and charcuterie boards), beer, wine and cocktails.

Fowlds Café, 3 Addington Sq, SE5 7JZ (020-3417 4500; Oval tube; Mon-Wed 7.30am-5pm, Thu 7.30am-10.30pm, Fri 7.30am-11pm, Sat 8.30am-5pm, Sun 9.30am-4pm).

Foxcroft & Ginger

Foxcroft & Ginger takes its name from its owners (Quintin Foxcroft and his flame-haired wife Georgina), who opened shop in 2010 after years of running other people's businesses. It's an all-day grazing spot, where you can enjoy a coffee and sandwich or a pizza with a glass of wine. Among the things that make it stand out are the spacious downstairs seating area with comfortable sofas (plus good wifi) and its relaxed ambience.

In addition to fine Monmouth coffee and leaf tea (Chash Tea), F&G have a passion for bread which is baked on the premises daily. It's made with a sourdough base and includes rye, ciabatta, focaccia or 'plain' sourdough (you can buy a loaf to take home), as well as providing the base for some seriously good pizzas. F&G also make their own croissants and muffins, and a range of enticing cakes and pastries.

Great British food with an original twist made from locally-sourced ingredients – the only thing it's bad for is your waistline! There are two other outlets in Old Street and Whitechapel.

Foxcroft & Ginger, 3 Berwick St, W1F 0DR (020-3602 3371; http://foxcroftandginger.co.uk; Piccadilly Circus tube; Mon 8am-7pm, Tue-Fri 8am-10pm, Sat 9am-9.30pm, Sun 9am-7pm).

The Gallery Café

The Gallery Café is a tranquil neighbourhood refuge housed in a handsome Georgian building in Bethnal Green (near the Museum of Childhood). It's part of St Margaret's House Settlement, a unique charitable organisation that provides working space, support and opportunities to community organisations and other charities in Tower Hamlets in East London.

The café serves a tasty selection of homemade vegan and vegetarian food (large portions) including all-day breakfasts, rolls, sandwiches, ciabattas, pizza and pasta, with most produce sourced locally. They also offer mouth-watering cakes, including a range of cupcakes, muffins and lemon drizzle cake, super coffee and a choice of teas. It's a light and airy, cosy sanctuary during the winter with a lovely bright conservatory area, and even better in summer when its sun-trap terrace and gardens – with big wooden tables and parasols – come into their own.

The café has a new art exhibition each month from an up-and-coming artist and is part of the First Thursdays initiative (www.firstthursdays.co.uk) that showcases original art, culture and events after normal opening hours on the first Thursday of each month.

The Garden Café, Garden Museum, 5 Lambeth Palace Rd, SE1 7LB (020-7401 8865; http://gardenmuseum.org.uk/page/cafe; Lambeth N tube or Waterloo tube/rail; Mon-Fri 10.30am-4.30pm, Sat-Sun 10.30am-3.30pm).

The Garden Café

The Garden Café at the Garden Museum is one of London's loveliest alfresco spaces, situated on the Thames next to Lambeth Palace, almost directly opposite the Houses of Parliament. Managed by

talented chef Sorrel Ferguson, the café is the perfect retreat from the bustling outside world, where you can relax in the 17th-century-inspired knot garden while enjoying outstanding coffee and cake (baked fresh each morning) or a delicious seasonal vegetarian lunch.

In 2012 the Garden Café was ranked sixth by *Gourmet* magazine in its rating of the 'world's top 10 museum restaurants', along with the likes of the Michelin-starred Nerua at the Guggenheim Bilbao and restaurants at The Hermitage in St Petersburg and the Musée d'Orsay in Paris.

This highly-rated oasis specialises in vegetarian food, including soups, salads, tarts and splendid cakes – try the scrummy orange, almond and rosemary cake. Lunch is served from noon to 3pm, while on Sundays

Duchess of Cornwall

the focus is on 'all-day' afternoon tea. The vegetarian (and often vegan) lunch menu changes daily depending on what's in season or available from the museum's vegetable patch.

The Garden Café, Garden Museum, 5 Lambeth Palace Rd, SE1 7LB (020-7401 8865; http:// gardenmuseum.org.uk/page/cafe; Lambeth N tube or Waterloo tube/rail; Mon-Fri 10.30am-4.30pm, Sat-Sun 10.30am-3.30pm).

Ginger & White

Since opening in Hampstead in 2009, Ginger & White has become *the* place for locals seeking good coffee; it's so successful that there's now a second café in Belsize Park. G&W is owned by food stylist Tonia George and restaurant managers Nick and Emma Scott, who were dismayed by the dearth of decent coffee shops in Hampstead. They also wanted somewhere that celebrated artisan food from British producers, so in addition to an excellent flat white (using Square Mile beans) you can fill up on breakfast classics (served all day), cakes, pastries, sandwiches and salads. Weekend brunches offer exciting concoctions such as roasted chorizo, avocado, lime and rocket on toasted ciabatta; smoked mackerel, fennel and Jersey Royal salad; and pear and polenta cake.

Inside there's a communal table and cool, vintage-inspired décor, but the pavement tables are the most highly prized and great for people watching. It's a child-friendly venue, so if you're allergic to kids you might want to check out the decibels.

Friendly atmosphere, good coffee, excellent food… G&W has it all. You can even take it home with you in the form of *The Ginger & White Cookbook*.

Ginger & White, 4A-5A Perrin's Ct, NW3 1QS (020-7431 9098; www.gingerandwhite.com; Hampstead tube; Mon-Fri 7.30am-5.30pm, Sat-Sun 8.30am-5.30pm).

Good Life Eatery

Run by two Americans – Yasmine Larizadeh and Shirin Kouros – the Good Life Eatery is one of the city's hottest new wave café-restaurants. Its *raison d'etre* is healthy eating, and everything on the menu is free-range, organic, sustainable, natural, etc. It's also delicious so you don't have to sacrifice flavour for nutrition.

The achingly trendy interior – exposed brick, glossy wood and state-of-the-art hardware – matches the fashionable food, which includes cold-pressed juices, protein-rich smoothies, wholesome salads and other super-food delights (try the avocado chilli on rye toast or open-faced teriyaki salmon). The prices are high but you're eating in Chelsea – maybe some of the gold dust will rub off on you…

Good Life Eatery, 59 Sloane Ave, SW3 3DH (020-7052 9388; www.goodlifeeatery.com; S Kensington/Sloane Sq tube; Mon-Fri 7.30am-8pm, Sat 8am-7pm, Sun 9am-6pm).

Gracelands Café

Gracelands is a cosy café run by Cecile and Nick (the chef), a couple whose passion for using only the best quality ingredients ensures excellent eating. The all-day breakfast menu ranges from full English to organic muesli and porridge, with eggs Benedict, Florentine and Royale available at weekends. For lunch there's a wide range of tasty sandwiches and salads, along with burgers, quiches and specials such as fiery jerk chicken, Thai vegetable curry and fish pie. The excellent coffee is from Caravan and there's also a selection of craft beers and a short wine list.

A family-friendly venue, Gracelands also offers a kids' menu and alfresco seating.

Gracelands Café, 118 College Rd, NW10 5HD (020-8964 9161; http://gracelandscafe.com; Kensal Gn tube; Mon-Fri 8.30am-5pm, Sat 9am-4.30pm, Sun 9.30am-3.30pm).

The Haberdashery

The perfect antidote to chain coffee shops, the Haberdashery is a quirky combination of gift/tuck shop and café. It serves up excellent coffee (Nude Espresso) and teas (W Martyn of Muswell Hill), plus hot chocolate, hot spiced apple juice, homemade cakes and pastries. And it has one of the best all-day breakfast/brunch menus in north London.

Breakfast treats include a traditional full English or 'veggie English', French toast, breakfast baguettes, eggs Benedict and oak-smoked salmon. For lunch you can choose from dishes such as Scandinavian meatballs, fishcakes and falafel, while from Thursdays to Saturdays it opens in the evenings as a cool bar with fantastic cocktails.

The Haberdashery, 22 Middle Ln, N8 8PL (020-8342 8098; www.the-haberdashery.com; Highgate tube/Crouch Hill rail; daily 9am-6pm).

Hand Made Food

Award-winning Hand Made Food in Blackheath Village is much more than just a café; it's also a delicatessen and *traiteur* (posh takeaway) where chefs develop their skills while creating delicious meals. You can take their food away – they specialise in outside catering – or eat in the bijou café, where the small space is supplemented by a few pavement tables.

The menu offers everything from breakfast to evening meals. Wherever possible, produce is free-range and seasonal, supplied mostly by small British growers and producers, many in southeast England. Dishes include fresh pâtés, pies and salads, mains such as Thai fish cakes and crispy pork belly, plus cakes, pastries and fine cheeses. Good value, too!

Hand Made Food, 40 Tranquil Vale, SE3 0BD (020-8297 9966; www.handmadefood.com; Blackheath rail; Mon 8.30am-5pm, Wed-Sat 8.30am-7pm, Sun 8.30am-4pm, closed Tue).

Hummingbird Café

A tiny, Antipodean-style hidden gem, pretty Hummingbird Café is a friendly neighbourhood eatery at the heart of the local community in Shepherds Bush. It's owned by a lovely couple, Lorraine (a Kiwi) and Brahim (from Morocco), whose food influences – not surprisingly – are drawn from around the globe. They

are passionate about their coffee (Ozone, Square Mile), speciality teas (Sherston Tea) and simple, flavoursome food, which is as organic and free-range as possible (including gluten- and wheat-free options). Food is also seasonal and locally and ethically sourced.

All-day brunch is the main draw, including home-baked mango, coconut and maple granola, egg specials (Benedict, Florentine and Royale), blueberry pancakes, spiced baked chorizo eggs, plus the usual heart-attack-on-a-plate cooked breakfast. For lunch there's a choice of fresh salads, tasty sourdough open sandwiches (such as slow-cooked Moroccan lamb, hot chorizo and pepper, and chipotle pulled pork) and a choice of daily specials. There's also

a good selection of cakes and pastries (some homemade), including raspberry and chocolate brownies, lemon and rosemary cake and banana bread. The café is licensed and offers some well-chosen wines and tasty craft beers.

Hummingbird Café, 1C Oaklands Grove, W12 0JD (020-8746 2333; www.hummingbirdcafe. co.uk/shepherds-bush; Shepherd's Bush Market tube; daily, summer 7.30am-7pm, winter 7.30am-5pm).

J+A Café

J+A Café occupies the ground floor of an old diamond-cutting factory at the rear of a maze-like East London yard. Simple and unpretentious, the large room has a warm and rustic feel with lots of natural light and exposed brick walls. Its centrepiece is a large refectory table, with smaller tables dotted around, while on sunny days you can sit in the tranquil courtyard.

The licensed café is run by sisters Johanna and Aoife (J+A) Ledwidge and the wholesome home cooking reflects their Irish roots. From artisan breads to organic meats, all produce is meticulously sourced from local suppliers whenever possible. Lunch choices include sandwiches, pies, quiches and salads – specials such as soups, pies and stews are advertised on a large blackboard – while bar snacks focus on simple small plates such as ham potato cakes, organic smoked salmon and dressed crab with soda bread. Not forgetting scrumptious cakes such as chocolate Guinness cake and Irish apple pie.

On Wednesday to Friday evenings J+A morphs into a romantic bar, with candles on the tables and inventive cocktails. Good value, friendly and a lovely atmosphere.

J+A Café, 1-4 Sutton Ln, EC1M 5PU (020-7490 2992; http://jandacafe.com; Barbican tube; Mon-Fri 8am-6pm, Sat-Sun 9am-5pm, Wed-Fri bar until 11pm).

Kensington Square Kitchen

Kensington Square Kitchen is a spacious café-restaurant (set over two floors) serving wholesome seasonal food, British-inspired and locally sourced (where

possible). The menu ranges from delicious homemade cakes and muffins to pies, salads and daily specials, all cooked on the premises by chef-patron Sara Adams and her team.

Breakfast ranges from healthy options such as homemade granola and the KSK signature porridge to heartier dishes such as a full English. At weekends the all-day brunch menu features some more unusual options such as wild mushrooms on toast with duck egg and watercress, and Turkish eggs with harissa yoghurt and sourdough. There are also themed supper clubs.

Kensington Square Kitchen, 9 Kensington Sq, W8 5EP (020-7938 2598; www. kensingtonsquarekitchen.co.uk; High St Kensington tube; Mon-Fri 8am-4.30pm, Sat 8.30am-4.30pm, Sun 9.30am-4pm).

The Kitchen@Tower

The Kitchen@Tower is a large, bright café next door to the historic All Hallows-by-the-Tower church, close to the Tower of London (two towers for the price of one!). It's a welcome oasis with a laid-back ambience and the bonus of a tranquil garden setting for sunny days.

The Kitchen is licensed and serves traditional British favourites, including full English breakfast, snacks, lunch and afternoon tea, with some veggie and vegan options. The extensive menu includes classic British fare such as shepherd's pie, fish and chips, liver and bacon and ham and eggs, as well as lighter dishes like cheese on toast or ploughman's lunch.

The Kitchen@Tower, Byward St, EC3R 5BJ (020-7481 3533; www.thekitchenattower. com; Tower Hill tube; Mon-Fri 8am-5.30pm, Sat 9am-5.30pm, Sun 10am-5.30pm).

Lantana Fitzrovia

The highly-rated, award-winning Lantana (an Australian flowering plant) café opened in 2008, since when it has gone from strength to strength and spawned others in Camden (see page 96) and Shoreditch. Lantana serves delicious coffee and is famous for its big Aussie-style breakfasts, lunches and weekend all-day brunches, not forgetting its excellent selection of baked goodies, which includes raspberry friands – a muffin-like cake – and cherry cake. It's licensed, too.

There's a cosy Antipodean atmosphere with wooden tables, mismatched chairs, white walls covered in art, and seating both indoors and outside (although never quite enough) – but it can get noisy at busy times.

Lantana Fitzrovia, 13 Charlotte Pl, W1T 1SN (020-7637 3347; http://lantanacafe.co.uk; Goodge St tube; Mon-Fri 8am-6pm, Sat-Sun 9am-5pm).

Leila's Shop

Owned by Leila McAlister, Leila's Shop is a bijou gem in Shoreditch; a combination of old-fashioned grocer and modern café. Farm-fresh fruit and veg is displayed outside in woven baskets, wooden crates and glazed bowls, while the rustic interior is piled high with seasonal produce and store-cupboard goodies.

The peaceful café is famous for its irresistible breakfast/brunch (served until 12.30pm) – you can't go wrong with Leila's signature dish of fried eggs with sage or crisp-fried Serrano ham (served in a cast-iron frying pan) and sourdough toast. There are also homemade preserves, muesli and yoghurt, or you can just fill up on delicious (Coleman) coffee, croissants and cake.

Leila's Shop, 15-17 Calvert Ave, E2 7JP (020-7729 9789; Bethnal Grn tube; Wed-Sat 10am-6pm, Sun 10am-5pm, closed Mon-Tue).

Lido Café

Situated in the grounds of Brockwell Lido in Herne Hill, the Lido Café serves award-winning food in a unique and beautiful setting. First opened in 1937, this Art Deco treasure is one of just a few London lidos remaining. Café-goers can sit by the pool on sunny days or enjoy the view from the light and airy dining room when the weather is less obliging.

The food is as good as the location – past winner of *Time Out* magazine's 'Best Park Café' award – and incorporates the best seasonal ingredients across a range of delicious dishes. Breakfast is a particular treat, whether you opt for eggs Benedict or blueberry pancakes with maple syrup, a classic 'full English' or granola with fruit compote and yoghurt. The coffee is reliably good as well.

Lido Café, Brockwell Lido, Dulwich Rd, SE24 0PA (020-7737 8183; www.thelidocafe.co.uk; Herne Hill rail; Sun-Tue 8am-5.30pm, Wed-Sat 8am-11pm).

Lisboa Patisserie

Lisboa Patisserie is a rare find on London's café scene: an authentic Portuguese café, without an Aussie or Kiwi in sight, selling scrumptious cakes and pastries to a loyal clientele.

Small and homely, its highpoints are the coffee – strong espresso (*bica*) and creamy latte (*galão*) – and its celebrated custard tarts (*pastéis de nata*) shown above. People travel from far and wide for these sweet delights, with their rich egg custard filling in a crisp puff pastry case. You may have to queue and share a table but the experience is worth it. And it's great value, too.

Lisboa Patisserie, 57 Golborne Rd, W10 5NR (020-8968 5242; Ladbroke Grove or Westbourne Pk tube; daily 7.30am-7.30pm).

Loafing

Occupying a lovely corner spot in Victoria Park Village, Loafing is a laid-back kind of place done out in shabby-chic décor that's offset by an impressive chandelier, antique mirrors and vintage china crockery (some of it for sale). When the sun obliges, there are outdoor tables in a small rear courtyard.

The stunning window display is enough to entice any cakeaholic with its tempting array of sweet treats, ranging from sponge cake and brownies to apple tart and lemon drizzle – there are gluten-free options, too. Loafing also does a nice line in savoury snacks and soups, toasted sandwiches and salads, most priced at less than a fiver, not forgetting excellent Monmouth coffee and hot chocolate.

Loafing, 79 Lauriston Rd, E9 7HJ (020-8986 0777; www.loafing.co.uk; Cambridge Heath/ London Fields rail; Mon-Fri 7.30am-6pm, Sat 8am-6pm, Sun 9am-6pm).

The London Particular

This attractive café-restaurant is named after a famous pea soup and offers classic English food with a modern twist. It employs the best seasonal ingredients – artisan breads, quality meats, free-range eggs and select British cheeses – and is a sociable place to eat as the food is served up at large communal tables.

On weekdays the menu switches from breakfast (try the eggs Benedict, merguez sausages and beef brisket) to lunch (sweet potato and leek cakes or baked eggs with chilli and sage), followed by coffee and cake; dinner is served Thu-Sat, and at weekends there's a delicious brunch. It's simple, convivial and homely, with a good selection of wines and beers.

The London Particular, 399 New Cross Rd, SE14 6LA (020-8692 6149; www. thelondonparticular.co.uk; New Cross rail; Mon-Wed, Thu-Sat 10am-10pm, Sun 10am-4.30pm).

Look Mum No Hands

One of the few places in London where you can have coffee and cake while getting your bike serviced, Look Mum No Hands is a café/bar, bike repair shop and events venue catering to the cool new breed of London cyclists. The café occupies a vast space with plenty of tables, excellent coffee by Square Mile and filling food – you can also get a beer or a glass of wine.

A cyclist's Mecca, it shows cycle sports (e.g. Tour de France) projected onto a huge screen, and has a workshop offering bicycle maintenance courses.

Look Mum No Hands, 49 Old St, EC1V 9HX (020-7253 1025; www.lookmumnohands.com; Barbican or Old St tube/rail; Mon-Fri 7.30am-10pm, Sat 8.30am-10pm, Sun 9.30am-10pm).

Lowry & Baker

A pretty little café in Notting Hill, Lowry & Baker has been a fixture on Portobello Road since 2010, serving some of the best breakfasts in west London. It's the perfect neighbourhood café with a staunch following, so much so that at weekends it's difficult to get a table.

The reasonably-priced menu is small but perfectly formed; everything is of the highest quality, including tasty soups, sandwiches, salads and other savouries – try the toasted sourdough with mashed avocado, poached eggs and smoked salmon. There's also a good selection of scrumptious cakes and pastries (delicious blueberry cheesecake and banana bread) and excellent Monmouth coffee. Friendly, cosy, good food and coffee – delightful!

Lowry & Baker, 339 Portobello Rd, W10 5SA (020-8960 8534; www.lowryandbaker.com; Ladbroke Grove tube; Mon-Sat 8am-4pm, Sun 10am-4pm).

Melrose & Morgan

Melrose & Morgan in chic Primrose Hill (there's another branch in Hampstead) calls itself a grocery shop, although it's far from your average corner store. M&M is an outstanding gourmet delicatessen and café, where you can enjoy breakfast, lunch or tea, and then pick up something special for supper. This grocer-cum-kitchen supplies artisan products and ingredients as well as freshly-prepared meals, for those who care about the quality of their food and can afford the very best. Some two-thirds of the food is made in-house in small batches and the rest is carefully sourced from local artisans and independent retailers.

M&M is the perfect retreat for a delicious breakfast, brunch or lunch. Hearty, filling savouries include a range of pies, tarts and frittatas, a good choice of salads and sandwiches, plus lunchtime specials and a

dish of the day – all prepared using top-quality, seasonal ingredients. For those with a sweet tooth, there's a good choice of pastries and cakes (try the dark chocolate Florentine tart) and excellent coffee. Not the cheapest place in town, but one of the very best.

Melrose & Morgan, 42 Gloucester Ave, NW1 8JD (020-7722 0011; www.melroseandmorgan. com; Chalk Farm tube; Mon-Fri 8am-7pm, Sat 8am-6pm, Sun 9am-5pm).

Milk

A wonderful combination of excellent coffee and Aussie-style food (from Lauren and Julian), Milk is a cool, laid-back Balham retreat where the friendly staff make you feel right at home while dishing up some of the best food in the area. As they say on their website: 'We make coffee. We bake

cakes. We cook you breakfast and play you our favourite records while we do it.' (Hopefully your favourite music includes deep house!)

The spacious, inviting interior is light and airy, with shabby-chic whitewashed brick walls and wooden tables.

The food and drink is carefully sourced, including coffee courtesy of Workshop (or possibly Koppi of Sweden), tea from Suki, organic juices from Heron Valley and delicious smoothies. The regularly-changing menu includes influences from all over with dishes such as Kurdish baked eggs with chorizo, spinach, *labneh* and Turkish dried chilli; poached eggs on sourdough toast with

dry-cured smoked bacon and Hollandaise sauce; sweetcorn fritters with grilled halloumi, smashed avocado, *kasundi* (tomato relish) and lime; and, of course, an awesome full English. Expect to queue for brunch at weekends.

Milk, 18-20 Bedford Hill, SW12 9RG (020-8772 9085; www.milk.london; Balham rail; Mon-Sat 8am-5pm, Sun 9am-5pm).

Minkies Deli

Minkies Deli is a renowned deli-café serving award-winning food in a beautiful, bright space (with outside benches for sunny days). Fresh seasonal ingredients are carefully sourced and all dishes prepared from scratch by chef and founder Doron Atzmon.

What better way to start your day than with Minkies' all-day breakfast of organic eggs (scrambled, fried or an omelette), organic back bacon or Scottish smoked salmon, toasted sourdough bread (baked in-house) and freshly-squeezed orange juice, all rounded off with coffee, tea or hot chocolate. For later, there's a range of homemade cakes (including award-winning triple choc brownies and wheat- and gluten-free receipes) plus charcuterie, cheeses, sandwiches, salads, soups and hot daily specials. A gastronomic goldmine!

Minkies Deli, 'Glasshouse', Chamberlayne Rd, NW10 5RQ (020-8969 2182; http://minkiesdeli. co.uk; Kensal Rise rail/Kensal Grn tube; Mon-Sat 8am-7pm, Sun 8am-5pm).

Monocle Café

This buzzy, striking Marylebone café (think Swedish sauna meets sushi bar) opened in 2013 and is a spin-off from Monocle magazine, the showcase of design consultant and publisher Tyler Brûlé (founder of Wallpaper).

As well as tasty, full-flavour Allpress coffee, there are Swedish pastries (from Fabrique bakery in Haggerston) and scrummy cakes from Lanka, a local Japanese-run tea room that fuses French baking with Japanese flavours such as green tea (see page 128). There's also an eclectic brunch/lunch menu, which includes Japanese and German breakfasts, chicken curry, Danish hotdogs, shrimp *katsu* sandwiches, *yakisoba* noodles and much more.

Monocle Café, 18 Chiltern St, W1U 7QA (020-7135 2040; http://cafe.monocle.com; Baker St tube; Mon-Wed 7am-7pm, Thu-Fri 7am-8pm, Sat 8am-8pm, Sun 8am-7pm).

Mouse & de Lotz

Opened in 2010, Mouse & de Lotz – named after owners Nadya Mousawi (Mouse) and Victoria Shard (nee de Lotz) – is a friendly neighbourhood café in Dalston serving healthy breakfasts, superb Square Mile coffee, homemade cakes and pastries, sandwiches, soups and savoury dishes.

Breakfast consists of toast, Bircher muesli, granola and pancakes rather than eggs and fry-ups, while lunch offerings include sandwiches (try the homemade hummus and roasted aubergine or mozzarella and green pesto, both served with tomato and rocket) and dishes such as roast mushrooms and warm goat's cheese on toast with salad, and smoked salmon on sourdough rye, horseradish, beetroot and rocket. Really tasty food at very reasonable prices.

Mouse & de Lotz, 103 Shacklewell Ln, E8 2EB (020-3489 8082; http://mousedelotz.com; Dalston Kingsland rail; Mon-Fri 8am-4pm, Sat 9am-4pm, Sun 10am-4pm).

The Natural Kitchen

Founded in 2007, the Natural Kitchen in Marylebone is one of London's best food shops, offering everything a committed foodie could desire: there are another four branches across the capital. The crowded pavement tables are witness to the Kitchen's enduring appeal, and there's a café upstairs.

The ground floor houses the shop counters, as well as tables where you can enjoy drinks and

light snacks. Upstairs there's a large, bright conservatory-style café with a laid-back atmosphere serving delicious breakfasts, including eggs every which way, organic porridge and granola with berries, and yogurt and Bircher apple muesli, plus a range of sandwiches, salads, and hot and cold main dishes. There's also a frozen yogurt bar.

The Natural Kitchen, 77-78 Marylebone High St, W1U 5JX (020-3696 6910; www. thenaturalkitchen.com; Baker St tube; Mon-Fri 7am-8pm, Sat 8am-7pm, Sun 9am-7pm).

New London Café

A lovely vintage-inspired café and organic food shop in Highbury, New London opened in 2011 and soon became a neighbourhood favourite. The wonderful interior, retro right down to the wallpaper, old school desks and retro music, has been designed to take you back to the golden era of the caff. There's also a cute little courtyard out back.

In addition to good Freetrade coffee, tea, juices and smoothies, New London is famous for its superb hearty breakfast/brunch menu that includes all the perennial favourites and more, plus a selection of cakes and pastries, sweet and savoury pancakes, tasty homemade burgers, a wide choice of sandwiches and delicious salads. All at bargain prices.

New London Café, 216 Saint Paul's Rd, N1 2LL (020-7354 7321; www.newlondoncafe.co.uk; Canonbury/Highbury & Islington rail; Mon-Sat 8am-6pm, Sun 8.30am-6pm).

The Nordic Bakery

Opened in 2007 by Finn Jali Wahlsten, this delightful Scandinavian-style café is a peaceful retreat; spacious and airy, minimalist but stylish, with a combination of wood-lined and deep blue walls. Golden Square is the original but there are two more Nordic Bakeries in W1.

The food is based on genuine Nordic recipes and ingredients and includes the house favourite cinnamon buns (and many other varieties of bun), plus delicious open sandwiches on rye bread topped with prawns, *gravlax*, pickled herring, hard-boiled egg and lingonberries. Cakes are scrumptious and the coffee is good and strong; if you want something different to drink, try the blueberry cordial. A star.

Nordic Bakery, 14A Golden Sq, W1F 9JG (020-3230 1077; www.nordicbakery.com; Piccadilly Circus tube; Mon-Fri 8am-8pm, Sat 9am-7pm, Sun 10am-7pm).

No 67, South London Gallery

The South London Gallery is almost as famous for its independent café-restaurant as it is for its art. Occupying a huge, bright and airy space, No 67 has two main dining areas, plus a garden with additional seating, where you can enjoy breakfast and lunch during the week and all-day brunch at weekends.

The robust seasonal menu includes small plates and mezze dishes as well as daily specials, sandwiches, and delicious coffee and cakes. In the evening it becomes a relaxed, bistro-style restaurant. A treasure – and the gallery's well worth visiting too!

No 67, South London Gallery, 67 Peckham Rd, SE5 8UH (020-7252 7649; http://number67. co.uk; Peckham Rye rail; Tue 8am-6.30pm, Wed-Fri 8am-11pm, Sat 10am-11pm, Sun 10am-6.30pm, closed Mon).

Ottolenghi

Yotam Ottolenghi's acclaimed eatery in Islington (opposite the Almeida Theatre) showcases his trademark Middle Eastern dishes: a beguiling marriage of explosive Mediterranean and Asian flavours in a palette of vibrant colours. It's one of the deli chain's few 'proper' café-restaurants, seating some 50 diners around communal tables in a cool, sophisticated environment.

Ottolenghi is open for breakfast, lunch and dinner, although bookings are only accepted at Upper Street for dinner, so if you fancy tucking into the legendary weekend brunch you need to arrive early. It's also a terrific place for vegetarians.

Ottolenghi, 287 Upper St, N1 2TZ (020-7288 1454; www.ottolenghi.co.uk; Highbury & Islington tube; Mon-Sat 8am-10.30pm, Sun 9am-7pm).

Patisserie Deux Amis

A pretty French café in Bloomsbury (just five minutes from King's Cross), Patisserie Deux Amis is a delightful place to stop for good coffee/tea and cake or a spot of lunch. The tranquil café – French country style with intimate little tables, plaster cherubs, etched glass mirrors and sage green paintwork – is an oasis in this frenetic part of town, and on fine days you can sit at one of the pavement tables.

There's a tempting display of delicious pastries, cakes, tarts, croissants and breads on the counter, plus tasty sandwiches (try the chicken, bacon, cranberry and mayonnaise baguette), quiches, soups and savoury *tartes* for lunch. The perfect sanctuary.

Patisserie Deux Amis, 63 Judd St, WC1H 9QT (020-7383 7029; Russell Sq tube; Mon-Sat 9am-5.30pm, Sun 9.30am-2pm).

Pavilion Café, Highgate Wood

O ccupying an idyllic space on the edge of ancient Highgate Wood, the Pavilion Café is popular with families and can be hectic at weekends. But its wisteria- and rose-clad terrace, plus a sea of outdoor tables (with umbrellas), makes it the perfect spot for a drink or lunch on a sunny day.

On offer is a wealth of savoury treats, including tasty soups, toasties, burgers, pastas, salads, filled pitta breads and mezze dips, plus a seasonal main course at weekends. For those who just want coffee/tea and a snack, there are delicious homemade cakes. Try the almond, lemon and polenta cake, blueberry muffins or push the boat out with afternoon cream tea.

Pavilion Café, Highgate Wood, Muswell Hill Rd, N10 3JN (020-8444 4777; Highgate tube; daily, summer 9am-9pm, winter 9am-3.45pm).

Pavilion Café, Victoria Park

Victoria Park – known colloquially as 'Vicky Park' – was London's first public park in 1845 and is still much loved by East End folk. Its old pavilion is now home to what is widely acknowledged to be one of London's best park cafés.

tea, to ensure that the fare stands out from the crowd.

Lunch ranges from fancy sandwiches (such as *'nduja* and *pecorino*) to burgers and salad. There's also excellent coffee (Monmouth) and tempting homemade cakes – the chocolate and marmalade is pretty unforgettable.

Pavilion Café, Victoria Pk, Crown Gate West, Grove Rd/Old Ford Rd, E9 7DE (020-8980 0030; Bethnal Grn or Mile End tube; daily 8am-4pm).

The Pavilion Café occupies a lovely domed glass building overlooking the lake, although in summer all the seating is outdoors on the terrace. It's a hearty (all-day) breakfast destination, offering both workaday and classic dishes from beans on toast to eggs Florentine, Benedict or Royale, all served in huge portions at reasonable prices. Owners Rob Green and Brett Redman use top-quality British ingredients such as rare-breed meat (Ginger Pig), Cotswold eggs and fine Ceylon

E Pellicci

Opened in 1900 and still run by the same family, Pellicci's is an East End institution. This king among caffs is a throwback to the golden age of café culture and has a wonderful Art Deco interior (Grade II listed). The profusion of lovely marquetry, stained glass, wood panelling and Formica tables make Pellicci's a rare example of the stylish Italian cafés that flourished in London in the inter-war years.

Punters flock here (the notorious Kray twins were regulars) as much for the atmosphere and decor as for the Italian hospitality and good tucker, prepared with pride every day by matriarch (and meatball queen) Maria. The fry-ups are as timeless as the premises – a full English of egg, bacon, sausage, mushrooms, tomatoes and a fried slice costs just £6 (veggie breakfast £5.50).

Other classic dishes include fish and chips, daily grills, Italian specials (spaghetti and meatballs) and toothsome desserts such as bread pudding, jam roly-poly, apple crumble and Portuguese custard tarts, and the prices are endearingly low. The freshly-squeezed orange juice and coffee are excellent, too.

If you're looking for tasty food, friendly efficient service, authentic atmosphere and excellent value, Pellicci's ticks every box. *Benissimo*!

E Pellicci, 332 Bethnal Green Rd, E2 0AG (020-7739 4873; Bethnal Grn tube; Mon-Sat 7am-4pm, closed Sun).

Persepolis

Owned by the indomitable Sally Butcher and her Iranian husband Jamshid, Persepolis in Peckham is much more than a food shop and café – it's an Aladdin's cave of all things Persian, from samovars to shisha pipes. But don't let the handicrafts distract you; this charming shop is a serious foodie haven.

Aiming to feed you from breakfast to supper, the colourful crazy café is a hidden treasure serving delectable vegetarian dishes created by food-author Sally, whose mission is to bring the flavours of Middle Eastern and Levantine cooking to south London.

Delicious mezze dishes (enough for two) served with warm bread and wraps form the bulk of the menu, with seasonally-inspired fillings such as halloumi, quince and caramelised celeriac. There's also baked sweet potato filled with Persian baked beans and halloumi, scrambled eggs with plantain and harissa (or dates and fragrant spices), and even a hotpot of the day. But make sure you leave room for a Persepolitan sundae: choose from Knickerbocker glory, saffron banana split, hot *paklava* meltdown (layers of fresh nutty pastry sweets muddled up with ice cream and toffee sauce) or the scrummy Turkish delight sundae.

Drinks are equally exotic, whether you opt for Turkish coffee, Afghan green tea, sour cherry juice or date and cardamom latte. Fantastic value, too!

Persepolis, 28-30 Peckham High St, SE15 5DT (020-7639 8007; http://foratasteofpersia.co.uk/the-cafe; Peckham Rye rail; daily 10.35am-9pm).

Petitou

Situated off bustling Bellenden Road in a 'gentrified' part of Peckham, charming Petitou occupies an old butcher's shop. The interior is all reclaimed scrubbed wood, flooded with light from huge picture windows. Outside there's a hand-built ceramic terrace, scattered with tables, adorned with planters and shaded by a grand old London plane tree – the perfect spot to meet, eat, drink and unwind.

Expect superior coffee and cakes (the lemon polenta cake and chocolate banoffee pie are highly recommended) and wholesome comfort food using seasonal produce. Perennial favourites include scrambled eggs, soups, quiches, salads (served with warm flatbreads) and sandwiches on granary bread. Petitou is fully licensed and serves a selection of wines and bottled beers.

Petitou, 63 Choumert Rd, SE15 4AR (020-7639 2613; www.petitou.co.uk; Peckham Rye rail; Mon-Sat 9am-5.30pm, Sun 10am-5.30pm).

Polo Bar

The Polo Bar is a 24-hour café close to Liverpool Street station that opened in 1953, although it's had a recent makeover; it doesn't look much from the outside but inside there are comfortable booths and tiled cream walls. It's the quality of the food that elevates the Polo above other caffs, and it really is also a bar with a 24-hour alcohol licence – so you can order a bottle of Cristal champagne to go with your 'full English'!

The coffee might not be the best but the grub is a cut above most other greasy spoons and includes excellent burgers, pies and sandwiches – and where else can you get a fry-up at 3am?

Polo Bar, 176 Bishopsgate, EC2M 4NQ (020-7283 4889; http://polo24hourbar.co.uk; Liverpool St tube/trail; open 24/7).

Queen's Wood Café

This non-profit community café is tucked away among 52 acres of ancient woodland in Haringey, and offers delicious organic, seasonal food (with lots of vegetarian options) in a child- and dog-friendly environment. Queen's Wood is a peaceful refuge from the hustle and bustle of the city, where you can chill out and enjoy a beer or a glass of wine with your meal, while the kids play on the Jungle Walkway.

You can even learn to play Himalayan singing bowls here – how many other cafés offer that? Very reasonable prices, too.

Queens Wood Café, Queens Lodge, 42 Muswell Hill Rd, N10 3JP (020-8444 2604; http:// queenswoodcafe.co.uk; Highgate tube; Mon-Fri 10am-4/5pm, Sat-Sun 9am-5/6pm).

Regency Café

The Regency Café in Pimlico is one of London's few remaining classic caffs. It dates from 1946 and still going strong, with original Art Deco tiles, Formica tables, fixed plastic chairs and old sporting photographs. In 2013 it caused quite a stir when it was named as one of the country's best cheap 'restaurants' on the Yelp website, proving we still have a healthy appetite for traditional British grub.

Here you can feast on dishes such as liver and bacon, steak pie with chips or apple pie with custard, washed down with a mug of builder's tea. But the big breakfasts are the star turn and cheap enough to make the Regency worth a detour.

Regency Café, 17-19 Regency St, SW1P 4BY (020-7821 6596; Pimlico/Victoria tube; Mon-Fri 7am-2.30pm, 4pm-7.15pm, Sat 7am-noon, closed Mon).

Riding House Café

The ultra-cool Riding House Café styles itself 'a modern all-day brasserie', offering breakfast, lunch, dinner, weekend brunch, Sunday lunch, and everything in between. There's even a separate bar with comprehensive cocktail and wine lists. There are individual place settings – try the cosy, retro orange banquettes – or you can sit at the grand communal refectory table; there's also a secluded dining room and lounge – not forgetting the bar.

Breakfast offerings include Scottish smoked salmon with scrambled eggs, eggs 'hussard' (with ox heart tomato, ham and spinach, plus bordelaise and hollandaise sauces), chorizo hash browns and Orkney bacon sandwiches, along with a 'full and proper English breakfast' (priced at £12.50). Also on the menu are cereals, porridge, fresh fruit, pancakes, pastries and a mouth-watering choice of juices and smoothies (served in old-fashioned milk bottles) with intriguing names. Try the Radio Flyer: watermelon, strawberries, lime, elderflower and a grind of black pepper.

The brunch, lunch and dinner menus bring on a broad range of dishes, from tapas-style small plates to full-sized brasserie mains and (on Sundays!) a choice of Sunday roast – or you can just have a coffee and cake or a cocktail. Fabulous.

Riding House Café, 43-51 Great Titchfield St, W1W 7PQ (020-7927 0840; www.ridinghousecafe.co.uk; Oxford Circus tube; Mon-Thu 7.30am-11.30pm, Fri 7.30am-midnight, Sat 9am-midnight, Sun 9am-10.30pm).

River Café

No, not that River Café – this is the original in Fulham (opposite Putney Bridge tube station), an old-fashioned caff offering British favourites at old-fashioned prices. The décor is stuck in a charming time warp: Vitrolite ceiling, blue and white tiles, seascape murals, wooden seats and Formica table tops, plus Juventus posters.

The owner is from Italy but you won't find fancy provincial Italian cooking at astronomic prices (à la the other River Café). The focus here is on traditional English breakfasts, generously portioned and reasonably priced, and good, honest, rib-sticking British grub, be it shepherd's pie or ham, egg and chips. Get stuck in!

River Café, 1A Station Approach, SW6 3UH (020-7736 6296; Putney Br tube; Mon-Fri 6.30am-3.30pm, Sat 6.30am-3pm, closed Sun).

Rose Bakery

Rose Bakery isn't a bakery at all but rather a classy café on the top floor of the cult designer label store, Dover Street Market. It's owned by Rose Carrarini – founder of the Villandry café-restaurant chain – who launched the Rose Bakery as an English teashop in Paris and brought it to London in 2007.

This popular concession at DSM specialises in delicious salads, soups, quiches, tarts and desserts, as well as the Bakery's famous cakes and pastries (be sure to try the carrot cake). You'll have to queue at peak times and may need to share the long communal table, but it's worth it.

Rose Bakery, Dover St Market, 17-18 Dover St, W1S 4LT (020-7518 0687; http://london. doverstreetmarket.com/dsmpaper/rose_bakery. html; Green Pk tube; Mon-Sat 11am-5pm, Sun noon-4pm).

The Russet

The welcoming Russet (bar/café/ restaurant) in Hackney – close to Hackney Downs – offers something for everyone: breakfast, brunch, lunch or an evening meal. It's the site canteen for Hackney Downs Studios, so alongside the healthy food there's an eclectic programme of arts, music, film, theatre and dance. The interior is a jumble of cast-off chairs, tables and sofas, and there's also an inviting alfresco seating area.

The inventive menu offers rustic seasonal food (including their take on Spanish tapas), which changes depending on what's available locally. There's also excellent coffee from Union Roasted, bread from the E5 Bakehouse (see page 167) and ale from London Fields Brewery.

The Russet, 17 Amhurst Ter, E8 2BT (020-3095 9731; http://eatworkart.com/the-russet; Rectory Rd rail; Mon 9am-5pm, Tue-Thu 9am-11pm, Fri 9am-12pm, Sat 10am-12pm, Sun 10am-11pm).

Sable d'Or

The Sable d'Or ('Golden Sand') is a continental-style café-patisserie in Crouch End (with another in Muswell Hill), producing some of the best cakes and pastries in north London. Indulge yourself in Viennoiserie, croissants (delicious almond croissants), cakes, tarts, blueberry cheesecake, brownies, chocolate gateau and more – and a huge variety of breads.

There's a cracking all-day breakfast menu, plus sweet and savoury crepes, soups, salads and sandwiches. The latter include grilled ciabatta, open sandwiches and brioche treats – the Brioche de Montagne (warm goat's cheese, garlic peppers, rocket, tomato, a dash of balsamic vinaigrette and pesto sauce) is a star turn. Drinks range from superior coffee and smoothies to 'power boost' blends. Magic!

Sable d'Or, 43 Crouch End Broadway, N8 8DT (020-8341 7789; www.sabledor.co.uk; Highgate tube; Mon-Fri 7.30am-6pm, Sat-Sun 7.30am-6.30pm).

Scandinavian Kitchen

The Scandinavian Kitchen was established in 2006 by Bronte (a Dane) and Jonas (a Swede) who, having failed to find authentic Scandinavian food in London, decided to import it themselves. Scandi food is simple, natural and honest, made with the staple produce of the land – they call it *husmanskost* (farmer's fare). It's also

delicious, although the fermented herring is definitely an acquired taste!

Sample the daily smorgasbord in their lovely café in Fitzrovia (you can't miss it – the shop frontage is pillar-box red) where they serve decent coffee (made with Monmouth beans) and a good range of teas, and bake delicious cakes and pastries such as Swedish cinnamon buns, *kladdkaka* (Swedish sticky chocolate cake, served with whipped cream) and apple cake. For lunch, there are mix-and-match salad combos (beetroot and apple, carrot and courgette, sweet potato and feta cheese), open sandwiches (try the rare roast beef with remoulade and horseradish on dark rye bread) and wraps (e.g. smoked ham and Scandinavian cheese), plus a soup of the day (always vegetarian). And of course they serve the ever-popular meatballs, and hot dogs with crispy onions.

Further temptations come in the form of Scandinavian groceries to take home, from dill-cured salmon to liquorice and lingonberry jam. Smaskigt!

Scandinavian Kitchen, 61 Great Titchfield St, W1W 7PP (020-7580 7161; www.scandikitchen. co.uk; Oxford Circus tube; Mon-Fri 8am-7pm, Sat 10am-6pm, Sun 10am-4pm).

Scooter Caffé

A hip little honeypot, the Scooter Caffé is located in a tiny former Vespa workshop near Waterloo station. It's chaotic and unpretentious – retaining much of its scooter-infused charm – with a small garden and good (often live) music.

Owned by Kiwi scooter fanatic Craig O'Dwyer, there's a definite two-wheeled theme going on but the café caters for all and is fun. The excellent coffee is from Londinium and food is limited to some exceedingly good cakes, but this place is all about the vibe: laid back during the day, it mutates into a cool, buzzy bar in the evenings.

Scooter Caffé, 132 Lower Marsh, SE1 7AE (020-7620 1421; Lambeth N/Waterloo tube/rail; Mon-Thu 8am-11pm, Fri 8am-midnight, Sat 10am-midnight, Sun 10am-11pm).

The Shepherdess

A nother traditional London caff, the unpretentious Shepherdess on City Road was a recent winner of the 'Best Builder's Breakfast in Britain', chosen by tradesmen on the www.mybuilder.com website. Jamie Oliver is a regular (his restaurant, *Fifteen*, is just around the corner).

Complete with the requisite plastic sauce bottles on each table, the 'Shep' serves a stonking British fry-up (eggs, bacon, sausages, tomatoes, mushrooms and hash browns) for

around £6 – not just one of the best in London (or even the world?) but fantastic value, too. There's also proper tea and coffee, an extensive sandwich menu, and traditional lunch dishes such as steak and kidney pie. Brilliant!

The Shepherdess, 221 City Rd, EC1V 1JN (020-7253 2463; Old St tube; Mon-Fri 6.30am-4pm, Sat 7.30am-3pm, closed Sun).

Snaps & Rye

Yet another of the wave of Scandi cafés popping up all over London, cosy Danish Snaps & Rye in Notting Hill is a treasure. Run by Jacqueline and Kell Skött, it serves delicious food and coffee (Nude Espresso) in a minimalist setting: white walls, blonde wooden tables and discreet art.

Healthy breakfasts include *skyr* (yoghurt), porridge and *tebirkes* (Danish 'croissants'), although it's the huge choice of tasty *smørrebrød* (open sandwiches on dark organic rye bread) that's the main draw. Tasty toppings include homemade gravlax, prawns, pickled herring, smoked duck, organic pork liver pâté, smoked eel, meatballs and much more. Lækker!

Snaps & Rye, 93 Golborne Rd, W10 5NL (020-8964 3004; www.snapsandrye.com; Westbourne Pk tube; Tue-Wed 8am-6pm, Thu-Sat 8am-11pm, Sun 10am-6pm, closed Mon).

The Spoke

The Spoke is large, bright neighbourhood café in Holloway specialising in good coffee (Union), tasty burgers and imaginative cocktails. This former pub allegedly has a cycling connection – hence the name – and has had a stylish makeover with shabby-chic, mismatched furniture and an open kitchen at the heart of the action.

The Spoke serves excellent coffee, homemade cakes and creative cooked breakfasts (try the poached eggs, chilli avocado and smoked salmon on toast), while the street-food inspired lunch menu includes pork shoulder sandwich, beef, chicken or prawn po' boy sandwiches (a Deep South classic) and the aforementioned burgers.

The Spoke, 710 Holloway Rd, N19 3NH (020-7263 4445; www.thespokelondon.com; Upper Holloway rail/Archway tube; Mon-Fri 7.30am-midnight, Sat 8am-midnight, Sun 8am-10pm).

Stamford Larder

Established in 2010 by Matthew Warren and Emily Johnson, the Stamford Larder – formerly the Upsy Daisy Bakery – owes some of its fame to winning the National Cupcake Championships in 2012. However, there's much more to this shop-cum-eatery than delicious cupcakes and 'cuptails' (alcoholic cupcakes – try the award-winning Mojito).

It's difficult to pigeonhole the Larder as it's a licensed café, coffee shop (organic Peruvian coffee) and tea room serving traditional afternoon tea. In addition to its divine cakes, it offers an extensive breakfast and brunch menu including organic granola and yoghurt, eggy classics (Benedict, Royale etc.), full English, soups, quiches, sandwiches and salads, plus daily specials.

Stamford Larder, 387 King St, W6 9NJ (020-0011 3387; www.stamfordlarder.com; Stamford Brook tube; Mon-Fri 8am-6pm, Sat 9am-6pm, Sun 9am-5pm).

The Table Café

The Table Café is one of Southwark's hidden gems. Occupying the ground floor of an anonymous architects' office, it consists of a large Scandinavian-style room with clean modern lines, floor-to-ceiling glass windows, communal oak tables and stools at the counter.

Chef Cinzia Ghignoni (an Angela Hartnett protégé) has created a modern menu that emphasises the restaurant's commitment to provenance, sustainable sourcing and quality British ingredients. The Table dishes up breakfast, lunch and evening meals (with live jazz nights on the second Thursday of the month), plus a weekend brunch that's good enough to lure foodies from nearby Borough Market. Tasty, value-for-money dining in SE1.

The Table Café, 83 Southwark St, SE1 0HX (020-7401 2760, http://thetablecafe.com, Southwark tube, Mon 7.30am-4.30pm,Tue-Fri 7.30am-10.30pm, Sat-Sun 8.30am-4pm).

Terry's Café

A traditional English café at the heart of Borough Market for over 30 years, Terry's is famous for its friendly service and honest home-cooking, using quality, locally-sourced produce

(much of it from the Market). Tea is just 20p a cuppa when served with food and coffee is by Monmouth, but what packs the punters in are the hearty super-sized fry-ups, headed by the The Works: Cumberland sausage, egg, bacon, bubble and squeak, black pudding, beans, tomatoes and mushrooms.

Lunchtime specials include toad-in-the-hole, traditional roasts, fish and chips, plus regulars such as ploughman's, gammon steak, beef burgers and homemade fish finger sandwiches.

Terry's Café, 158 Great Suffolk St, SE1 1PE (020-7407 9358; www.terryscafe.co.uk; Borough tube; Mon-Fri 7am-2pm, Sat 7.30am-noon, closed Sun).

Towpath

The Towpath has earned a stellar reputation for good coffee and delicious Mediterranean-inspired food – and has a prime position on Regent's Canal towpath. It's a narrow open-fronted café with tables by and even *on* the canal, courtesy of a floating pontoon.

Opened in 2010, this cool café attracts a bevy of passing walkers and cyclists but also entices custom from far and wide specifically to sample its excellent fare. This includes crunchy granola with yoghurt, fruit and maple syrup, eggs on sourdough toast and tasty grilled cheese sandwiches, plus tempting sweet delights such as truffle buns and olive oil and lemon cake.

Towpath, 36 De Beauvoir Crescent, N1 5SB (020-7254 7606; Haggerston rail; Tue-Wed, 8am-8pm, Thu-Fri 8am-9pm, Sat-Sun 9am-11pm, closed Mon and from Nov to March).

Tried & True

Tried & True in Putney specialises in all-day breakfast/brunch. In 2014 it scooped an award for the UK's Most Innovative Breakfast (Big Breakfast Awards) for its BBQ pulled pork Benedict: spice rubbed 15-hour roasted pork shoulder, tossed in

breakfast/café culture to west London with amazing coffee (Square Mile), Suki tea and delicious food, using the freshest ingredients to create original

twists on tasty classics. It's also licensed, serving beers from Camden Town Brewery and Kim Crawford Kiwi wines. God's own café!

Tried & True, 279 Upper Richmond Rd, SW15 6SP (020-8789 0410; www.triedandtruecafe. co.uk; Putney rail; Mon-Fri 8am-4pm, Sat-Sun 8.30am-4.30pm).

hickory hoisin sauce, served on homemade jalapeno cheddar cornbread, topped with two poached eggs, chilli butter and spring onions. And there's plenty more where that came from, including eggs Benedict house style, portobello mushrooms on seven-seeded toast with an optional poached egg, and buttermilk pancakes with seasonal compote, mascarpone and maple syrup.

Owned by Kiwi Rob Kelly – who wanted to create a cool local café just like the one round the corner from 'the (legendary) garage in Mt Eden, New Zealand – T&T brings a touch of Auckland's relaxed

Troubadour Café

Put your feet up at the legendary Troubadour Café – opened in 1954 – a multi-faceted café/wine bar/art gallery and live music venue. The bohemian 'Troub' hosted Jimi Hendrix, Joni Mitchell and Bob Dylan in the '60s and is still cluttered with paraphernalia from its hippie days. Nowadays though, it's one of London's most charming and relaxing hangouts, with an idyllic garden.

It puts emphasis on the provenance of its fare and its vast menu features brilliant breakfasts and lunches, including fresh salads, soups and 'one pot wonders', plus Troubadour classics such as omelettes, burgers, steaks and daily specials. The coffee's special, too.

Troubadour Café, 263-7 Old Brompton Rd, SW5 9JA (020-7370 1434; http://troubadour.co.uk; Earls Court tube; daily 9am-midnight).

Urban Gourmet

It may be tiny, but the Urban Gourmet café-deli in Wandsworth punches well above its weight, offering a huge choice of gourmet groceries, excellent coffee, scrumptious cakes and pastries (try the finger-licking Malteser cake from Flossy Cockles, a rich two-layer chocolate ganache sponge adorned with these moreish sweets), and tasty soups, salads and sandwiches. Special dietary needs are catered for with vegan savoury pastries and gluten-free cakes.

Gourmet groceries come from near and far and include artisan organic bread (Celtic Bakers), truffled salami from Italy, Bookham cheese (West Sussex), authentic pork pies and Slasher beer from a brewery called (really!) Piddle in Dorchester.

Urban Gourmet, 201 St John's Hill, SW11 1TH (020-3441 1200; www.urban-gourmet.co.uk; Wandsworth Town rail; Mon-Sat 9am-5pm, Sun 10am-4pm).

White Mulberries

Nestling in a quiet corner of St Katharine Docks – minutes from the Tower of London – is White Mulberries, a cosy, friendly café with panoramic views over the marina. It serves excellent Allpress Coffee, including drip-to-order filter coffee and AeroPress brews. Food-wise there are scrummy cakes and pastries, such as chocolate melts, walnut and cappuccino cake and caramel macarons, plus brilliant breakfasts and tasty savoury treats.

But the biggest draw is the view – and on sunny days you can sit outside on the boardwalk and watch the world go by. Lovely.

White Mulberries, D3 Ivory House, St Katharine Docks, E1W 1AT (www.whitemulberries.com; Tower Hill tube; Mon-Fri 7.30am-5pm, Sat 8am-6pm, Sun 8.30am-6pm).

Wilton Way Café

Wilton Way Café in Hackney is unusual in that it's also home to London Fields Radio, a unique local radio station (see website), and the walls serve as a gallery for local artistic talent. Quirky, comfortable and laid back, the Wilton serves excellent coffee (Climpson) and tasty, simple food using produce from local suppliers.

Favourites include organic Bircher muesli with apple, honey and Greek yoghurt; avocado on sourdough toast with lemon and chilli flakes; grilled chorizo ciabatta with piquillo peppers and rocket; and grilled Portobello mushrooms on garlic toast with goat's cheese and rocket. There's also a good selection of baked temptations, including oven-fresh croissants and scrummy cakes and biscuits.

Wilton Way Café, 63 Wilton Way, E8 1BG (www. londonfieldsradio.co.uk/the-café; Hackney Central rail; Mon-Fri 8am-5pm, Sat 8am-6pm, Sun 9am-6pm).

You Don't Bring Me Flowers

An unusual combination of florist and café, You Don't Bring Me Flowers (named after the Neil Diamond song) has been a fixture on Staplehurst Road in Hither Green (close to the station) for over ten years. It's arranged over two floors, with the florist downstairs and an intimate living room upstairs hosting the homely café, jam-packed with vintage paraphernalia including a huge

card board, assorted lamps, artwork and comfortable chairs. There's also a small patio area out front. To add to the relaxing ambience, the owner Lynne plays lovely background music on her (vinyl) record player.

The café serves Fairtrade coffee courtesy of a '60s Gaggia machine, loose-leaf teas (served in vintage teapots) and fruit juices,

along with a good choice of homemade cakes (delicious lemon drizzle cake and cupcakes), tarts, pastries, flapjacks, sandwiches, soups and more.

The shop also sells tea paraphernalia and foodie delights such as classic preserves, jams and chutneys, honey and hot pepper jellies – not forgetting the beautiful flowers and bouquets. And there are monthly writers' nights, film nights and other events. A magical place.

You Don't Bring me Flowers, 15 Staplehurst Rd, SE13 5ND (020-8297 2333; www. youdontbringmeflowers.co.uk; Hither Gn rail; Tue-Fri 8am-6pm, Sat 9am-6pm, Sun 10am-5pm, closed Mon).

2. Coffee Shops

Over the last few decades coffee shops in Britain – and London in particular – have been brewing up a storm, initiated in large part by an influx of enterprising folk from Down Under, home of the great flat white. There's been a wave of artisan coffee roasters and neighbourhood coffee shops launched by Antipodean entrepreneurs (and others), creating some (much-needed) stiff competition for the capital's Italian coffee bars and ubiquitous American coffee chains.

Independent coffee shops are fuelled by their single-minded passion for coffee; beans are carefully sourced – often roasted in-house – and brewed by skilled baristas. This usually distinguishes them from cafés, which generally place more emphasis on the food, although many cafés also serve excellent coffee and coffee shops often offer an extensive food menu. You'll usually also find homemade cakes, pastries and sandwiches, often accompanied by a selection of hot and cold dishes that wouldn't be out of place in a good restaurant; many are licensed, too.

This chapter features over 80 of London's best independent coffee shops, which have helped transform the city's coffee scene into a multi-billion pound market.

The first London coffee revolution was in the late 1600s and early 1700s, when hundreds of coffee houses played host to caffeine-fuelled debate, wheeler-dealing and gossip-mongering, along with some serious business (Lloyd's of London started life in a coffee house).

Alchemy Café

Alchemy are one of the new breed of coffee importers/roasters dedicated to providing customers with exceptional coffee from around the world, including Colombia, Costa Rica, Ethiopia, Guatemala and Rwanda. A showcase for their coffee, Alchemy Café is where they serve up to five different brews on an ever-changing roster, including espresso, hand-brewed filter and cold-brewed coffees – these guys are purists, so don't expect a cappuccino or flat white here! They also offer a selection of cakes, pastries and light lunches, but espresso is king.

Alchemy sell coffee, plus all the equipment and accessories needed to brew and drink it, and also offer workshops, service and support.

Alchemy Café, 8 Ludgate Broadway, EC4V 6DX (020-7329 9904; www.alchemycoffee. co.uk; St Paul's tube; Mon-Fri 9am-5pm, closed weekends).

Allpress Espresso

A popular artisan roastery café in buzzy Shoreditch, Allpress serves perfect coffee and tasty grub. Established by Kiwi Michael Allpress and Sydney chef Tony Papas in 2010, the café greatly expanded awareness of how coffee should taste among both coffee drinkers and café owners, many of whom now source their coffee from Allpress. The food menu is simple – a selection of breakfast plates and sandwiches

– but it's the coffee that takes centre stage.

The roaster can be seen in action during the week, while the freshly-roasted blends and single origin coffees can be purchased for home use. You can also attend a class on how to make the perfect espresso.

Allpress Espresso, 58 Redchurch St, E2 7DP (020-7749 1780; http://uk.allpressespresso. com; Shoreditch High St rail; Mon-Fri 8am-5pm, Sat-Sun 9am-5pm).

Artigiano

Artigiano is a cool coffee and wine bar in the City (close to St Paul's Cathedral) serving some of the city's best speciality coffee, using beans roasted exclusively for them by Origin Coffee. There's plenty of seating inside the slick interior, with exposed brick walls, stone floors, hanging lamps, wooden tables and stools, plus additional seating outside.

During the day Artigiano offers a variety of cakes, pastries, tarts, freshly-made baguettes, sandwiches, wraps, salads and other savouries – many baked in-house – plus natural juices and smoothies, while in the evening it becomes a trendy wine bar serving fine wines, craft beers and delicious cocktails (plus live music Thursdays).

Artigiano, 1 Paternoster Sq, EC4M 7DX (020-7248 0407; www.artigiano.uk.com; St Paul's tube; Mon-Tue 7am-9pm, Wed-Fri 7am-10pm, Sat-Sun 10.30am-6pm).

Artisan

Occupying a large minimalist corner spot with huge picture windows in Stamford Brook, Artisan is one of the new wave of independent coffee shops taking over the city, thanks to our Antipodean cousins. It's run by real enthusiasts who worship the bean and even run artisan courses for coffee geeks (see www.artisancoffeeschool.co.uk).

Morning starts with the delicious smell of freshly-brewed coffee (Allpress) and breakfast goodies, including granola, porridge and smoked salmon on focaccia. There's a good choice of cakes and pastries to go with your morning coffee (try the lemon and rosemary or chocolate and Guinness cake), while for lunch there are seasonal soups, salads, tarts and a wide selection of hearty sandwiches. There are other branches in Ealing, East Sheen and Putney.

Artisan, 372 King St, W6 0RX (020-3302 1434; www.artisancoffee.co.uk; Stamford Brook tube; Mon-Fri 7am-6pm, Sat 8am-6pm, Sun 8.30am-6pm).

Association Coffee

While claiming to be all about coffee, Association also offers a decent choice of tea, hot chocolate and organic juices in its beautifully designed City café (subtle lighting, natural wood, bare brick, etc.). But coffee (Has Bean/Square Mile) takes pride

of place here, with their regular espresso supplemented by guest brews or single origin coffees served at their brew bar, where you can also sample different coffee-making methods such as Aeropress, V60 and Syphon. There's also healthy breakfast fare (no fry-ups) such as granola, muesli, yoghurt, scrummy pastries and cakes, and a small selection of homemade sandwiches.

Association sell coffee and home brewing equipment, and offer free advice on coffee selection and home-brewing methods.

Association Coffee, 10-12 Creechurch Ln, EC3A 5AY (020-7283 1155; www. associationcoffee.com; Aldgate tube; Mon-Fri 7.30am-5pm).

The Attendant

One of London's most unique cafés, the Attendant occupies a former gentlemen's public convenience (toilet), built around 1890 and mothballed in the '60s. After two years of planning and restoration, it opened in 2013 as a tiny café, reached via steps descending below a splendid wrought iron canopy. The attendant's office has been converted into a kitchen and the original porcelain urinals revamped into a coffee bench, with green seating to match the original Victorian floor tiles.

It isn't, however, just a novelty attraction; the Attendant was runner up as 'Best Coffee Shop in London 2013' (www. londonlifestyleawards.com) and serves excellent (Caravan) coffee, gourmet sandwiches, salads and delicious cakes.

The Attendant, 27A Foley St, W1W 6DY (020-7637 3794; www.the-attendant.com; Goodge St tube; Mon-Fri 8am-6pm, Sat 9am-6pm, Sun 10am-5.30pm).

Bambuni

A lovely delicatessen and coffee shop in Nunhead, southeast London, Bambuni isn't the most obvious place to get a delicious flat white, but its coffee (Volcano) is up there with the best. Creating the deli-café was a labour of love for owner Huey, who did most of the refurbishment himself; it features polished wooden floors, white walls, spotlights and plenty of tables (with wifi and power outlets for your laptop and tablet). There's even a heated courtyard.

There's a great selection of cakes and pastries to go with your coffee and if you fancy lunch then Huey knocks up fantastic sandwiches which you can chase with super ice-cream (from Ice Cream Union). Bambuni is fully licensed, so you can even enjoy a craft beer – there are over 100 on offer – or a glass of wine with your lunch.

While you're here, why not take home some goodies (many of which can be purchased by weight or volume like in the good ol' days)? There's bread, cheese, charcuterie, Volcano coffee, chocolate, pork pies, fruit juices, granola, sauces, pasta, olive oil, wine, beer and much more. Huey also plans to hold events such as tapas evenings, beer tastings, film and bar nights. A foodies' treasure trove!

Bambuni, 143 Evelina Rd, SE15 3HB (020-7732 4150; www.bambuni.co.uk; Nunhead rail; Tue-Sat 9am-5.30pm, Sun 10am-4pm, closed Mon).

Bar Italia

Treat yourself to a coffee at Bar Italia, a family-run business founded in 1949 by Lou and Caterina Polledri and passed on down through three generations; first to their son Nino, who took over the reins in the '70s, and then to his children Antonio, Luigi and Veronica, who now run it alongside their Little Italy restaurant next door

A Soho institution, Bar Italia serves excellent Italian coffee and delicious pastries and cakes, and service is always with a smile. It's open around the clock – the alfresco tables are the perfect place for people watching on a sunny afternoon.

Bar Italia, 22 Frith St, W1D 4RP (020-7437 4520; www.baritaliasoho.co.uk; Tottenham Court Rd tube; open 24-7).

Barossa Fulham

Styling itself a coffee house and Australian kitchen, laid-back and friendly Barossa Fulham is a ray of sunshine in west London, serving divine coffee (Caravan) and delicious food. This attractive little café has a small front room and a larger back room where the serious eating goes on.

The food is seasonal, fresh and very tasty. All-day breakfast includes a Bondi brekkie (the Oz take on a full English), while lunch offers a kangaroo  steak sandwich and crab cakes with chilli and lime, and there's spiced lamb and mint burger and sticky toffee pudding on the dinner menu. A stand-out star and reasonably priced, too.

Barossa Fulham, 277 New King's Rd, SW6 4RD (020-7751 9711; http://barossafulham.com; Parsons Grn tube; Mon-Fri 8am-5pm, Sat 9am-5pm, Sun 9am-4pm).

Birdhouse

An Aussie-Cuban-owned coffee bar in Battersea, Birdhouse is a tranquil little hideaway, painted in shades of grey with flashes of canary yellow, scattered with reclaimed furnishings and sporting a bird-themed picture wall.

The faultless coffee is from Climpson, made with love and obvious skill, partnered with superior baked goods (such as warm banana bread, ANZAC biscuits, brownies, lamingtons, chocolate cake and friands), lovely breakfast items, freshly-baked paninis and tasty Cuban tea sandwiches called *bocaditos*, which literally translates as 'little bites'. Friendly staff and efficient service – every neighbourhood should have a Birdhouse.

Birdhouse, 123 St John's Hill, SW11 1SZ (020-7228 6663; Clapham Junction tube/rail; Mon-Fri 7am-4pm, Sat-Sun 9am-5pm).

Blend

Blend (also called Local Blend) opened in Harringay in 2013 (there's a newer branch in Notting Hill) and has been hailed as one of the best café/bars in north London. The relaxing space has a lively atmosphere and stylish Scandinavian design, including lovely reclaimed parquet flooring.

Blend styles itself a café, wine and cocktail bar – serving martinis all day – along with superb Climpson coffee, delicious homemade cakes and pastries (try the cherry Danish), and imaginative sandwiches. It's an excellent venue for brunch with a menu offering everything from granola to a veggie tomato curry. It mutates into a bistro in the evenings.

Blend, 587 Green Lanes, N8 0RG (020-8341 2939; www.localblend.co.uk; Turnpike Ln tube; Mon-Fri 8.30am-5pm, Sat 9.30am-5pm, Sun 10am-5pm).

Bread & Bean

Opened in 2011, Bread & Bean is a cosy little coffee shop in Archway, offering excellent coffee (Union's Revelations blend). It occupies a corner site with large windows, lots of wood, copper lamp fittings and quirky décor, including a framed section of bare brick wall behind the counter.

B&B's food ranges from fabulous breakfasts, including a full English ('breakfast for champions'), pancakes with bacon and maple syrup ('transatlantic breakfast'); and chorizo, potatoes and scrambled eggs with sourdough ('breakfast for lovers'). There are also sandwiches, jacket potatoes, soup and salad of the day, plus the inevitable array of cakes and pastries, many made on the premises. They serve an excellent cuppa as well.

Bread & Bean, 37 Junction Rd, N19 5QU (020-7263 0667; Archway tube; Mon-Fri 7.30am-6pm, Sat-Sun 8.30am-6pm).

Brickwood

Yet another of the wave of welcoming Antipodean cafés that have taken root in London in recent years, hip and homely Brickwood in Clapham (opposite Clapham Common tube station) is a large green-fronted café over two floors with a rustic interior (brick and wood – like it says on the tin!) and the bonus of a lovely courtyard out back.

As you'd expect there's excellent coffee (Caravan), good tea (Suki Tea), fresh fruit juices and super food, including a comprehensive brunch menu served daily until 3pm (try the smashed avocado with chorizo and poached eggs on sourdough), cakes and pastries, toasties, sandwiches, wraps and salads. There's a second branch in Balham.

Brickwood, 16 Clapham Common S Side, SW4 7AB (020-7819 9614; www.brickwoodlondon. com; Clapham Common tube; Mon-Fri 7am-6pm, Sat-Sun 9am-6pm).

Brill

Brill – slogan: Music, Coffee, Bagels – in buzzing Exmouth Market began life as a music shop (Clerkenwell Music) and although it's now a coffee shop the new owner (Jeremy Brill) has retained the music element, selling new and used CDs and some vinyl.

However, coffee (Union) and food – particularly bagels with smoked salmon, cream cheese, ham, hummus, etc. – account for most of the turnover. There's also a good choice of homemade cakes and pastries, and some irresistible breakfast/brunch options. Friendly staff, reasonable prices, good coffee, food and music – Brill is… brill!

Brill, 27 Exmouth Mkt, EC1R 4QL (020-7833 9757; Angel tube; Mon-Fri 7.30am-6pm, Sat 9am-6pm, Sun 10.30am-5pm).

Brooklyn Coffee

Okay, East London isn't exactly Brooklyn – although one of the co-owners *is* from Brooklyn – but Brooklyn Coffee is a great place to get your caffeine fix in Spitalfields. The monochrome exterior could be in Bond Street, while the striking compact and minimalistic interior has a polished concrete bar and a monochrome colour palette, a wooden floor and a few window seats.

Brooklyn uses Caravan beans served with soy or even almond milk (very NY) – the iced coffees are also good. A simple glass display case contains a tempting selection of cakes (try the Oreo brownies) and pastries, and there are also fancy Mast Bros (E2) chocolate bars on offer.

Brooklyn Coffee, 139 Commercial St, E1 6BJ (www.brooklyncoffee.co.uk; Shoreditch High St rail; Mon-Fri 7am-5pm, Sat-Sun 8am-5pm).

Browns of Brockley

Browns (named after the owner Ross Brown, whose pug Ludd is the café's mascot) is a gem of a neighbourhood coffee bar occupying a prime position opposite Brockley railway station. The shop's light and cosy interior features white walls, communal wooden tables, benches and comfy sofas, with laid-back, friendly staff serving perfect flat whites – rated by many as the best coffee south of the river – made with Square Mile beans.

However, where Brown's really excels is the quality and variety of its food. In addition to the superb selection of baked treats in the window (try the cinnamon doughnut muffins or greengage and lavender friands), it offers an unrivalled choice of baguettes (Flourish Bakery), toasted bagels (Brick Lane Bagels) and croissants filled with gastro goodies. The latter include pastrami and gherkin;

provolone, ham and tapenade; Parma ham, tomatoes and cheese; brie and cranberry; halloumi, red pepper, rocket and onion jam; slow-roasted lamb shoulder with broad bean hummus, mint and pomegranate; and more.

On Thursday nights the café is open late for 'Pizza Thursdays' with wood-fired pizzas and craft beers from the Magic Rock Brewing Company.

Browns of Brockley, 5 Coulgate St, SE4 2RW (020-8692 0722; www.brownsofbrockley.com; Brockley rail; Mon-Fri 7.30am-3pm, Sat 9am-5pm, Sun 10am-4pm).

Café Viva

A pretty independent coffee shop (opened in 2012) on Choumert Road in Peckham, Café Viva is a small but peaceful haven with a duck-egg blue exterior, white walls, exposed brick, a concrete floor, fresh flowers and colourful art. In addition to excellent rich and smooth coffee from Volcano – some of the best in the area – there's a good selection of teas and infusions, superb smoothies and fresh juices.

The homemade and locally sourced food menu – displayed on chalk boards – offers a selection of cakes and pastries, all-day breakfast including banana bread with Greek yoghurt and honey or fruit and nut granola with berry compote, toasted croissants, baps stuffed with bacon or chorizo, fried egg, roast tomato and rocket (there's a veggie version with mushroom), bagels (lovely smoked salmon and cream cheese), and freshly-made soups and toasties – all served on mismatched vintage crockery. Free wifi, good value – viva Café Viva!

Café Viva, 44 Choumert Rd, SE15 4SE (020-7639 2922; www.cafeviva.co.uk; Peckham Rye rail; Tue-Fri 7.30am-5pm, Sat-Sun 9am-5pm, closed Mon).

Caffè Vergnano 1882

Part of a small chain, Caffè Vergnano was a past *What's On* magazine 'Coffee Shop of the Year' and brews some of the best coffee anywhere in London – but then it is Italian owned (by three generations of baristas).

It's worth coming here for the location alone, comfortable and stylish, with alfresco seating for when the weather behaves, and full of history. Staple Inn was built in 1545 and was one of the few buildings to survive the Great Fire in 1666, only to be bomb damaged in 1944. The building was restored after the war but went into steady decline until being rescued by Luciano Vergnano to become the jewel of a coffee shop you see today.

When you want a real Italian coffee – whether it's an Americano, espresso, latte, macchiato or cappuccino – this is the place to come (just don't ask for a flat white!). Vergnano also serves delicious croissants (try the cheese, tomato and herb), cinnamon rolls, ricotta cheesecake, *torta della nonna* (custard pie with pine nuts and almonds) and much more. The perfect place to get your caffeine kick.

Caffè Vergnano 1882, Staple Inn, 337-338 High Holborn, WC1V 7PX (020-7242 7119; http:// caffevergnano1882.co.uk; Chancery Ln tube; Mon-Fri 7am-7pm, Sat 8am-5pm, Sun 8.30am-4pm).

Campbell & Syme

Founded in 2014, Campbell & Syme in East Finchley is both a coffee shop and roastery, sourcing its beans from far and wide. Passionate about coffee, they offer both espresso-based drinks and hand-brewed methods such as v60, Kalita Wave, Chemex and Aeropress – and they use organic milk.

The large, friendly café is dominated by the beautiful (Dutch) blue Giesen W6 coffee roaster, but it isn't all about coffee. There's also tea, hot chocolate, milkshakes, sandwiches and scrumptious cakes, muffins and macarons, baked on-site by Claire Jury of La Dinette, plus sourdough bread from Holt's Bakery.

Campbell & Syme, 9 Fortis Grn, N2 9JR (07977-514054; http://campbellandsyme.co.uk; E Finchley tube; Mon-Thu 7.30am-2pm, Fri 7.30am-4pm, Sat-Sun 9am-4pm).

Ca'puccino

An upmarket Italian 'coffee house and kitchen' near Sloane Square, Ca'puccino is the creation of Giacomo Moncalvo and is part of a chain extending across London (six branches) and Italy. No bland brand, Ca'puccino is passionate about coffee, serving its signature blend of beans roasted in-house. The interior is slick and stylish with white leather chairs, although the pavement tables are the prize place on sunny days.

There's a huge breakfast menu, plus excellent coffee, tea and juices, and an all-day menu offering Italian appetisers, salads, pasta dishes, paninis and focaccias, plus a vast range of irresistible desserts (delicious *gelati*) and pastries. It's licensed, too. Pricy but worth a visit.

Ca'puccino, 138A King's Rd, SW3 4XB (020-7036 0555; www.ca-puccino.com/location/ca-kingsroad; Sloane Sq tube; Mon-Fri 9am-7pm, Sat-Sun 10am-7pm).

Carter Lane Coffee House

A lovely little coffee house tucked away down a side street close to St Paul's Cathedral, Carter Lane produces some of the best coffee in the City on its handsome Synesso Hydra machine. Using Climpson's espresso blend as its main offering, the friendly Italian baristas also do a mean decaf espresso, delicious hot chocolate and iced latte.

CL offer a range of delicious pastries (super croissants), sandwiches, cakes (brownies, cupcakes) and cookies, including some delicious gluten- and dairy-free treats. They also sell a selection of Climpson beans, including their house blend. A little gem.

Carter Lane Coffee House, 50A Carter Ln, EC4V 5EA (020-7248 9493; www.carterlane-coffee. co.uk; St Paul's tube; Mon-Fri 7.30am-4pm, closed weekends).

Chairs & Coffee

Owned by cheerful Italians Roberto and Simone, Chairs & Coffee opened in 2013. A coffee bar by day and wine bar by night, the interior is fairly standard coffee/ wine bar rustic chic – bare brick, white walls and wooden tables – or it would be if it wasn't for the chairs hanging from the ceiling!

The delectable coffee is roasted in-house and made on a beautiful vintage Faema E61 built in 1963. There's also iced coffee, hot chocolate, organic *matcha* green tea (made with powdered green leaves), fresh juices, delicious cakes and pastries, plus plenty of eggy treats and toasted sourdough sandwiches for breakfast/brunch.

Chairs & Coffee, 512 Fulham Rd, SW6 5NJ (020-7018 1913; www.chairsandcoffee.co.uk; Fulham Broadway tube; Tue-Wed 8am-6pm, Thu 8am-10pm, Fri 8am-11pm, Sat 9am-10pm, Sun 9am-6pm, closed Mon).

Cinnamon Coffee Shop

Opened in 2012, Cinnamon is a great little neighbourhood coffee shop on the corner of Cinnamon Lane and Wapping Lane (not far from Tobacco Dock), with a lovely selection of homemade cakes. The shop has two small seating areas, including

a peaceful rear room with a large table and comfy armchairs and beanbags for those who like to linger over their coffee, perhaps with a newspaper from the rack, something from the book exchange or while surfing the net (there's free wifi and power points). There are also a few tables and chairs outside for sunny days.

Cinnamon offers a wide choice of excellent coffees (Monmouth) – try the cinnamon or *stavccino*, a Nutella-flavoured cappuccino – including iced coffee, with no extra charge for soya milk, cream or added flavours. There's also hot chocolate, fruit frappes and milk shakes. Food includes an above-average range of cakes and pastries – including carrot, summer fruits, mocha and red velvet cakes, plus croissants, muffins and millionaire's shortbread – and hot and cold savoury dishes (such as lasagne) for lunch.

Cinnamon Coffee Shop, 103 Wapping Ln, E1W 2RW (020-7702 2323; www. cinnamoncoffeeshop.co.uk; Wapping rail; Mon-Fri 7am-7pm, Sat 9am-6pm, Sun 9am-5pm).

Climpson & Sons

Climpson (the name came from the old butcher's shop the business inherited) was founded by Ian Burgess, who was inspired by five years spent drinking coffee in Australia. One of London's pioneer coffee roasters supplying many of the city's best coffee bars,

Climpson has its flagship café in Hackney's Broadway Market and, as you would expect from coffee masters, it's something of a mecca for coffee enthusiasts, offering a range of brew methods while exploring the best flavour profiles and extraction techniques. (For information about the roastery, see www.climpsonsarch.com.)

Established in 2002 and recently refurbished, the rustic café has whitewashed walls and ceilings, bare floorboards, plain wooden benches (inside and outside) and low tables, while a blackboard graphically explains the strength and taste of the available coffees and how they're made. The breakfast and lunch menus use locally-sourced produce whenever possible and the café bakes many of its own cakes, pastries and quiches in-house – but it's the coffee that headlines here.

There's a comprehensive selection of beans for sale, in addition to a variety of home-brewing equipment, so you can recreate the Climpson magic at home.

Climpson & Sons, 67 Broadway Mkt, E8 4PH (020-7812 9829; www.climpsonandsons.com; London Fields rail; Mon-Fri 7.30am-5pm, Sat 8.30am-5pm, Sun 9am-5pm).

Coffee Circus

The antithesis of the mega chains, Coffee Circus is a quirky, characterful coffee shop in Crouch Hill. The delightful interior has the air of an old-fashioned tea room – they offer a large selection of fine loose-leaf teas as well as coffee – with mismatched rustic furniture, a solid wood counter, bare floorboards, musical notes on the wallpaper, local art on the walls, and a dresser packed with coffee, tea and teapots behind the counter.

In addition to excellent coffee (beans from Union Hand Roasted among others – you can buy some to take home) and the aforementioned interesting selection of teas, you can indulge in hot chocolate, freshly-squeezed juices, plus a good choice of cakes and pastries. The short breakfast menu includes organic granola, baskets of individual patisseries, croissants, boiled eggs with soldiers, eggs Benedict, *croque madame* (*croque monsieur* with a fried egg*)*, muffins, and toast with artisan jams, while lunches include light salads, soups, vegetarian dishes (such as garlic mushrooms on toast) and a selection of tasty sourdough sandwiches.

Coffee Circus also operates two colourful coffee wagons (see website) at Camden Stables market, where the business started.

Coffee Circus, 136 Crouch Hill, N8 9DX (020-8340 8221; www.coffeecircus.com; Crouch Hill rail/Highgate tube; Mon-Fri 8am-6pm, Sat-Sun 9am-6pm).

Coffee Jar

Opened in 2013 by Maria, a refugee from banking (now poorer but happier!), Camden's Coffee Jar is a treasure: small, intimate and clearly a labour of love. The interior has just ten seats (there are a few more outside) and is as rustic as you can get, with the counter, tables and stools made from what looks like reclaimed scaffolding planks, offset by white walls.

But what Coffee Jar lacks in grandeur it more than makes up with it marvellous coffee (organic Monmouth beans), hot chocolate, and a fantastic range of (mostly) homemade baked goodies and tasty sandwiches. Add friendly service and free wifi and you've a delightful place to sit and watch the world go by.

Coffee Jar, 83 Parkway, NW1 7PP (07956-032741; www.kamden.co.uk; Camden Town tube; Mon-Fri 7.30am-5.30pm, Sat-Sun 9am-5.30pm).

Coffee Plant

Located in the heart of Portobello Road opposite the Electric Cinema, this is one of the increasing number of coffee bars/shops operated by a coffee roaster: Acton-based Coffee Plant offers the UK's largest range of certified organic and Fairtrade coffees from Guatemala, Mexico and Peru. Originally opened in 1997, the café moved to its current location in 2004 and still serves the best coffee in the area, particularly the delicious flat whites.

Coffee Plant offers teas, smoothies and the usual range of cakes, pastries, snacks, toasted sandwiches, etc., but its widespread fame rests with its superb freshly-roasted coffee, which you can also buy to brew at home.

Coffee Plant, 180 Portobello Rd, W11 2EB (020-8453 1144; www.coffee.uk.com; Ladbroke Grove tube; Mon-Sat 7am-5.15pm, Sun 9am-4.30pm).

The Coffee Works Project

One of three independent coffee shops owned by Peter Theoklitou (the others are in Blackfriars Rd and Leadenhall Market), the friendly Coffee Works Project was voted 'Best Café in Islington' in the 2014 *Time Out* Love London awards. The bright room with huge picture windows is industrial meets shabby-chic – white walls, reclaimed chairs and tables, old coffee crates and a vast rustic wooden bar – and there's a lovely courtyard garden out back.

Dedicated to serving superb coffee (Has Bean with milk from Northiam Dairy) on its beautiful Slayer machine, delicious premium teas (Waterloo) and delectable hot chocolate (Rococo), CWP is also acclaimed for its artisan food mostly made fresh on-site using seasonal produce from independent artisan suppliers. There's a wide selection of homemade cakes (try the ginger and

cardamom or banana and chocolate) and pastries from the Little Bread Pedlar, plus a range of sandwiches, salads, and cheese and charcuterie boards.

The Coffee Works Project, 96-98 Islington High St, N1 8EG (020-7424 5020; http:// coffeeworksproject.com; Angel tube; Mon-Fri 7.30am-6pm, Sat 9am-6pm, Sun 10am-5pm).

The Counter Café

Established in 2009, the Counter Café is located in the Stour Space Gallery (www.stourspace.co.uk): a huge ramshackle community arts centre on an industrial estate in Hackney Wick. The location may not sound too inviting, but the independent café and coffee roastery offers panoramic views of the River Lee Navigation canal and

the Olympic Stadium (just 100m away). It's a bright, laid-back café occupying a large inviting space with lots of seating, and has the bonus of a fantastic outdoor terrace (pontoon) on the canal.

Run by siblings Tom and Jess from Auckland, the Counter Café does perfect coffee, delicious cakes and pastries, soups, salads, historic pies and their world-famous

(at least in Hackney!) homemade tomato relish. But what draws the crowds is the epic brunch menu – one of the best in town – which includes a big Kiwi breakfast (sausage, chorizo, bacon, garlic mushrooms, new potatoes, eggs, toast and loads more). There's a vegetarian version and, for smaller appetites, scrambled eggs, bacon sandwiches, Turkish eggs, French toast, homemade muesli, etc. You can also buy beans to take home.

The Counter Café, 7 Roach Rd, E3 2PA (07834-275920; http://counterproductive.co.uk; Hackney Wick rail; Mon-Fri 8am-5pm, Sat-Sun 9am-5pm).

Craft Coffee

Experienced coffee masters Jamie and Emily – best-known for their Maltby Street coffee cart – are the brains behind Craft Coffee in bustling Shoreditch. The

minimalist but homely bar is all white walls, wooden counters and exposed copper piping (echoing its former life as a gallery) and, in pride of place, a lovely La Marzocco Linea coffee machine. It also has a small rear garden.

Unlike most coffee shops, Craft Coffee regularly rotate the beans used in their outstanding coffees; they are supplied by some of London's best roasters, including Alchemy, Caravan, Notes, Nude Espresso and Workshop. Food includes a small selection of delectable cakes (salted chocolate brownies, doughnut muffins) from Beas of Bloomsbury, filled croissants and sandwiches.

Craft Coffee, 68 Sclater St, E1 6HR (www.craft-coffee.co.uk; Shoreditch High St rail; Mon-Fri 8am-5pm, Sat-Sun 10am-5pm).

Curators Coffee Gallery

Opened in 2014, this is the second branch of Curators Coffee (the original is in Callum St, EC3) and is an interior designer's caffeine dream. A high-ceilinged room bathed in natural light, it has a stunning dark wood bar and white walls, one covered in honeycomb tiles in shades of grey-black which mirror the lovely floor.

Curators is dedicated to great-tasting coffee (Nude Espresso), affirmed by two blackboard coffee menus – classics and curated. Food includes cakes from Bittersweet bakeries, pastries from Yeast Bakery (fantastic croissants) and bread from Sally Clarke's bakery. There's also a selection of freshly-made ciabatta sandwiches, toasted sandwiches and salads, plus a fantastic weekend brunch menu.

Curators Coffee Gallery, 51 Margaret St, W1W 8SG (020-7580 2547; www.curatorscoffee.com; Oxford Circus tube; Mon-Fri 7.30am-6.30pm, Sat-Sun 9am-6pm).

Department of Coffee and Social Affairs

Formerly the Speakeasy Espresso & Brew Bar, this is one of nine branches of the Department of Coffee and Social Affairs chain, located just off Carnaby Street in tranquil Lowndes Court. The chain roasts its own coffee, which you can buy for home use, along with coffee-making equipment.

The bright, Scandi-style café is split between the ground floor and basement, with an espresso bar upstairs and a brew bar downstairs. In addition to a huge selection of speciality coffees, there's a range of quality teas and irresistible cakes (the chocolate cherry cake is wonderful), pastries and sandwiches from some of London's best bakers.

Department of Coffee and Social Affairs, 3 Lowndes Ct, W1F 7HD (020-7434 3340; http://departmentofcoffee.com/locations/carnaby-street; Oxford Circus tube; Mon-Fri 8am-7pm, Sat 9.30am-8.30pm, Sun 10am-7pm).

Dose Espresso

Owned and operated by James Philips, Dose Espresso is a one-man artisan espresso bar serving City folk with ethically-sourced coffee. It's supplied by Square Mile, sourced from farms practising biodiversity, and finished with organic milk.

Dose also makes splendid sandwiches – including a terrific bacon, lettuce and tomato – fresh salads, warming porridge, and toast with a variety of toppings such as homemade pesto, Vegemite or sliced tomato/avocado. Sweet treats are supplied by Arianna of Bittersweet Bakers, while bread and French pastries are sourced from the Seven Seeded Bakery and made with organic flour.

Dose Espresso, 70 Long Ln, EC1A 9EJ (020-7600 0382; http://dose-espresso.com; Barbican tube; Mon-Fri 7am-5pm, closed weekends).

Embassy East

Opened in 2013 by ex-Flat White baristas (Chris, Lehi and Tommy) with some 30 years' experience between them, Embassy East quickly established itself as one of Hoxton's best coffee bars. The simple, warm and inviting interior has exposed brick, white walls, shiny black floor, wooden tables with low green stools, exposed lighting, a small open kitchen in the back, and a rough-hewn wooden bench in the huge picture window.

The coffee (Workshop) is predictably superb, with enough choice to please any coffee aficionado. The short menu offers granola, porridge and eggs in various ways for breakfast, with appetising salads, sandwiches, soup and tasty toasties for lunch.

Embassy East, 285 Hoxton St, N1 5JX (020-7739 8340; www.embassyeast.co.uk; Haggerston/Hoxton rail; Mon-Fri 9am-6pm, Sat 10am-6pm, Sun 10am-5pm).

The Espresso Room

The tiny hole-in-the-wall Espresso Room in Bloomsbury is a shrine to espresso, which is made with consummate skill using beans from Square Mile (and others). Established in 2009 by self-confessed coffee geek Ben, it serves some of the best speciality coffees in town – including a super flat white – in a friendly and relaxed neighbourhood environment.

Despite its bijou size (there's just a central bar and a few benches) and small menu – soup of the day, sandwiches and some delectable cakes from Bea's of Bloomsbury (see page 121) – the Espresso Room has a loyal following. If the weather's fine try to grab one of the small tables outside.

The Espresso Room, 31-35 Great Ormond St, WC1N 3HZ (07760-714883; www.theespressoroom.com; Russell Sq tube; Mon-Fri 7.30am-5pm, closed Sat-Sun).

Exmouth Coffee Company

Founded in 2012 by coffee geek Jam and masterchef Eddie, the Exmouth Coffee Company roast their own coffee (Square Mile) and make most of their food in-house. Located on Whitechapel High Street (next door to Whitechapel Gallery – there's no name above the door), the relaxed and cosy

café offers lots of seating and industrial-chic décor: white tiled walls, black and white hexagonal tiled flooring, bare brickwork, wrought iron table stands with wooden tops and funky lamps.

The coffee is delicious – the house blend consists of Colombian, Brazilian and Honduran coffees, with beans from Papua New Guinea and Ethiopia used for 'slow' coffee – but the main draw here is the food. We defy anyone who's even slightly peckish to bypass Exmouth with their irresistible window display and counter piled high with freshly-baked cakes, pastries, paninis, muffins, flat-bread sarnies, filled croissants, soups, salads and quiches – and everything tastes every bit as good as it looks.

The food has North African influences (all meat is halal), with highlights including croissants with spinach and goat's cheese, mozzarella or pastrami in flat bread, tomato and avocado salad, and fantastic cherry almond tart. Exceptional!

Exmouth Coffee Company, 83 Whitechapel High St, E1 7QX (020-7377 1010; www. exmouthcoffee.co.uk; Aldgate East tube; daily 7am-8pm).

Federation Coffee

Buzzing Brixton Market is one of London's best eating and drinking destinations (and a great place to shop for food). It's also the home of Federation Coffee, Antipodean owned and operated and one of the best coffee shops in south London. Federation

roast their own coffee, using an ever-changing blend of coffees from Brazil, Ethiopia, El Salvador and Sumatra, and make all their own fresh food. The vast

menu includes over 100 sweet and savoury options – changing daily – all made in their own kitchen (also in the market). Try the super flat white or mocha accompanied by a cherry coconut slice or some moreish cheesecake.

People flock to this attractive café which is a good place to catch up on your email or surf the web, chat with friends or simply hang out and watch the characters that frequent Brixton Village drift by. There are only around a dozen tables, so you may have to share, but the locals are a friendly bunch. Excellent service, relaxed neighbourhood atmosphere, and good coffee and food in one of London's most cosmopolitan areas.

Federation Coffee, Unit 77-78, Brixton Village Mkt, Coldharbour Ln, SW9 8PS (http://federationcoffee.com; Brixton tube; Mon-Fri 8am-5pm, Sat 9am-6pm, Sun 9am-5pm).

The Fields Beneath

Named after a local history book about Kentish Town by Gillian Tindall, The Fields Beneath is a charming, friendly neighbourhood coffee bar – bare brick, Moroccan tiles, wooden floor – located in a railway arch beneath Kentish Town West railway station.

Sit at the large communal table (or outside) and enjoy superb coffee from Square Mile, Nude Espresso and others. There's a lavish display of pastries and cakes – lovely croissants (try the almond), yummy doughnuts (jam, custard, rhubarb and rose) and divine beetroot chocolate cake – plus tasty sausage rolls, toasties, soups and sandwiches, mostly sourced from small local suppliers. As good a coffee shop as you'll find in north London.

The Fields Beneath, 52A Prince of Wales Rd, NW5 3LR (020-7424 8838; Kentish Town West rail; Mon-Fri 7am-4pm, Sat 8am-5pm, Sun 9am-5pm).

Fitzrovia Coffee Bar

Located just off Regent Street in upmarket Fitzrovia, this is the fourth outlet from Workshop Coffee (see page 116), one of the city's leading roasters. The lovely understated exterior conceals a beautifully-designed sleek interior, with a parquet floor, burnished brass, eclectic furnishings, richly-upholstered chairs, a vast iridescent Madagascan granite bar and pearl blue highlights (which includes the cups), plus a

secluded seating nook in the rear.

As you'd expect, the coffee is superb, with an espresso-based menu alongside filter offerings through Aeropress and Fetco CBS brewers. The food menu is short and sweet: simple baguette sandwiches made in-house and a selection of pastries, muffins and brownies sourced from Yeast, Little Bread Pedlar and Sally White.

Fitzrovia Coffee Bar, 80A Mortimer St, W1W 7FE (www.workshopcoffee.com/pages/fitzrovia-coffeebar; Oxford Circus tube; Mon-Fri 7am-7pm, Sat-Sun 9am-6pm).

Fix Coffee

Fix on Whitecross Street (there's a second Fix on Curtain Road, EC2) occupies a large converted pub with a cool, laid-back atmosphere. The décor is mostly minimalist – white walls and exposed brick, bare floorboards, exposed light bulbs plus a few chandeliers – but an abundance of tables and old leather chesterfields makes it the perfect place to relax (there's also free wifi and lots of power points).

The Fix folk serve superb Climpson coffee (a special blend made exclusively for them), hot chocolate, smoothies and frappes, plus a selection of pastries and cakes, including vegan and gluten-free specialties. But it's the coffee and sofas that pull in the punters.

Fix Coffee, 161 Whitecross St, EC1Y 8JL (020-7998 3878; www.fix-coffee.co.uk; Barbican tube; Mon-Fri 7am-7pm, Sat 8am-pm, Sun 9am-7pm).

Flat White

Established in 2005, Flat White was one of the trailblazers that introduced Antipodean coffee culture to deprived Londoners, and it's been a favourite destination ever since. The flat white coffee – stronger, smaller and less milky than a latte, less froth than a cappuccino – is one of the best things to come out of Oz since Kylie. It's made using a Square Mile single origin blend that changes every few months (you can buy some to take home).

The food menu is small (but tasty) and the décor and seating basic – try to bag a seat outside in summer – but the coffee's superb!

Flat White, 17 Berwick St, W1F 0PT (020-7734 0370; www.flatwhitesoho.co.uk; Oxford Circus/ Tottenham Ct Rd tube; Mon-Fri 8am-6pm, Sat-Sun 9am-6pm, Sun 9.30am-6pm).

Fork Deli Patisserie

Fork Deli is a friendly café/coffee shop/patisserie/deli in Bloomsbury (close to Russell Square), serving delicious Monmouth coffee and quality loose-leaf tea (Tea Pigs). It has free wifi, a selection of newspapers and magazines, and plenty of seating in its homely interior.

Fork serves a good selection of cakes and pastries baked on site – try the moreish gluten-free chocolate and toffee brownies or scrumptious orange and almond cake – plus an ever-changing lunch menu offering a choice of salads, sandwiches, quiches and fresh soups (many vegetarian). If that's not enough, there's an extensive range of gourmet goodies – including organic bread, mouth-watering cheeses, cured meats and pasta – to take home.

Fork Deli Patisserie, 85 Marchmont St, WC1N 1AL (020-7387 2860; www.forkdeli.co.uk; Russell Sq tube; Mon-Fri 7.30am-7pm, Sat-Sun 9am-4pm).

Four Corners

A chic coffee shop behind Waterloo railway station, Four Corners is a travel-themed café decorated with maps of the world and globes, with a loyalty card in the form of a miniature passport. The quirky café is fronted in shades of pistachio green, while the smart interior is painted in greys and whites, with travel-related literature on the walls, a long bar, and ample tables and chairs.

It serves excellent coffee from Ozone, loose-leaf tea from Yumchaa (see page 137), irresistible cakes and pastries from Balthazar, tapas from Brindisa, and a small selection of paninis and soups. It's also licensed and serves tea and coffee infused spirits!

Four Corners, 12 Lower Marsh, SE1 7RJ (020-8617 9591; www.four-corners-cafe.com; Waterloo or Lambeth N tube; Mon-Fri 7.30am-6.30pm, Sat 9am-5pm, closed Sun).

FreeState Coffee

Now you have even more reason to visit delightful Sicilian Avenue in Bloomsbury, as FreeState Coffee is just a few steps away from this elegant arcade. The café occupies a spacious shop with huge picture windows and an eclectic assortment of tables and pews.

The folks at FreeState use Fairtrade coffee from Union, who source their beans from around the globe; the house espresso is dark-roasted foundation blend (a mixture of Guatemalan, Indonesian and Indian beans) and there's also a 'guest espresso'. For the peckish there's a good selection of sandwiches, pastries, croissants, cakes, salads and quiches.

FreeState Coffee, 23 Southampton Row, WC1B 5HA (020-7998 1017; www.freestatecoffee. co.uk; Holborn tube; Mon-Fri 7am-7pm, Sat-Sun 9am-6pm).

Golborne Deli

A lovely, homely espresso bar and deli in west London, close to Portobello Road, Golborne Deli serves fantastic coffee, tea and food. Established in 2002 and under new owners since 2011, the rustic café has been restyled, giving it a more laid-back atmosphere, with mismatched furniture and art on display (there's also some alfresco seating).

The owners are passionate about their coffee – each cup is served with a cool mini-milk bottle and a little amaretti biscuit – and the food is also superb. For breakfast there's everything from freshly-baked croissants and pastries to toasted ciabatta with scrambled eggs and smoked salmon. Lunch choices range from soups, salads and sandwiches to tasty Mediterranean dishes.

Golborne Deli, 100 Golborne Rd, W10 5PS (020-8969 6907; http://golbornedeli.com; Westbourne Pk tube; Mon-Sat 7.30am-7pm, Sun 9am-6pm).

Goswell Road Coffee

Part of the small but cool and edgy Brick Lane Coffee (aka Street Coffee) chain, Goswell Road Coffee's wacky interior includes comfy sofas, neon signs, wall doodles and ceiling lamp shades made from plastic coffee cups! However, it isn't just about style; when it comes to coffee, Goswell Road can more than hold its own, brewing excellent coffee using organic and Fairtrade beans from Papua New Guinea.

Food, including a selection of vegan and gluten-free items, is mostly from local suppliers and includes salads, sandwiches, soups, cakes and pastries (almond croissants to die for!). There are also newspapers and magazines to read, free wifi and good music.

Goswell Road Coffee, 160-164 Goswell Rd, EC1V 7DU (020-7490 7444; www. bricklanecoffee.co.uk; Barbican tube; Mon-Fri 7am-7pm, Sat-Sun 8am-7pm).

Grind Coffee Bar

A popular independent coffee bar in Putney since 2010, Grind is owned by Kiwi Dave Dickinson, a professional drummer in a former life. It serves excellent coffee – a blend of beans from Brazil, Papua New Guinea and Peru – roasted exclusively for Grind by London Coffee Roasters.

Grind is renowned for its awesome breakfast/brunch menu which features poached/scrambled eggs on sourdough, blueberry pancakes, mushrooms on toast, Kiwi bacon and egg pie, and much more. There are also luscious homemade cakes (white chocolate and raspberry muffin, lemon slice, banana bread), plus a range of tasty burgers, salads, wraps and sandwiches.

Grind Coffee Bar, 79 Lower Richmond Rd, SW15 1ET (0845-862 9994; www.grindcoffee. com; Putney Bridge tube; Mon-Fri 7am-6pm, Sat-Sun 8am-6pm).

Haggerston Espresso Room

Looking a little like a second-hand furniture showroom, Haggerston Espresso Room (or HER for short) is a thriving café off Kingsland Road close to Haggerston station. The huge room is furnished with a jumble of mismatched vintage furniture, including comfy armchairs and sofas, with a few benches outside for sunny days.

HER serves seriously good Climpson coffee and tasty food, including a selection of mouth-watering cakes and pastries (try the almond croissants and blueberry cheesecake), 'sexy toast' – sourdough toast with cream cheese, honey and cinnamon – organic porridge, soup and a range of sandwiches, tarts and frittatas. It's a lovely place to chill out, read the free magazines or surf the web.

Haggerston Espresso Room, 13 Downham Rd, N1 5AA (020-7249 0880; Haggerston rail; Mon-Fri 7.30am-6pm, Sat 9am-6pm, Sun 10am-6pm).

Iris & June

Named after the grandmothers of co-founder Jodie (a Kiwi – what else!) who inspired her love of food, Iris & June is a vibrant artisan coffee shop in the heart of Victoria. It was designed from the ground up and is all clean lines, concrete floors, cool white furnishings and oodles of space.

The awesome coffee is from Ozone, made on a beautiful La Marzocco Strada machine, and there's also a good range of teas, hot chocolate, herbal infusions and juices. Most food is prepared fresh on site using premium ingredients and includes a mouth-watering array of breakfast, lunch (salads, sandwiches, quiches, frittatas) and baked treats. Grandma would approve!

Iris & June, 1 Howick Pl, SW1P 1WG (020-7828 3130; www.irisandjune.com; Victoria tube/rail; Mon-Fri 7.30am-5.30pm, Sat 8.30am-4pm, closed Sun).

Kaffeine

Another of London's ubiquitous Antipodean coffee shops (are there any baristas left Down Under?), Kaffeine opened in 2009 and has been mopping up awards ever since. Like most of London's independent cafés, excellent coffee (Square Mile) is a given, but Kaffeine is also noted for

its excellent food which includes tasty salads, sandwiches (try the yummy souk lamb) and muffins. It also does a nice line in cakes and pastries such as chocolate brownies, Portuguese custard tarts and ANZAC biscuits (naturally!).

Friendly, buzzy and creative, Kaffeine also runs coffee courses for aspiring amateur baristas. There's a second branch in Fitzrovia.

Kaffeine, 66 Great Titchfield St, W1W 7QJ (020-7580 6755; http://kaffeine.co.uk; Great Portland St tube; Mon-Fri 7.30am-6pm, Sat 8.30am-6pm, Sun 9am-5pm).

Lantana Camden

From the same Aussie stable as Lantana Fitzrovia (see page 36), Lantana Camden − formerly the Ruby Dock Café − is a welcome peaceful oasis amid the hustle and bustle of hip Camden Market. The large, bright café − huge windows, white walls, wooden benches and table tops − offers plenty of alfresco seating for people-watching.

It serves superb coffee (Square Mile and others) and tea and a good selection of tasty tucker, including a breakfast menu, a variety of homemade cakes and pastries, soups, toasted sandwiches, filled croissants, sausage rolls and creative salads. There's also a selection of beer and cocktails.

Lantana Camden, 45-46 Middle Yard, Camden Lock Pl, NW1 8AF (020-7428 0421; http://lantanacafe.co.uk; Camden Town tube; daily 9am-5.30pm).

Leyas

Leyas source their excellent coffee from a wide variety of roasters including Union Hand Roasted, Square Mile, Notes Roastery, Nude Espresso, Alchemy and Drop Coffee, so while you never know what you're going to get, you *do* know it'll be awesome! The attractive façade – with a huge picture window (the prized spot to sit) – conceals a small ground floor with seating and counter.

The main seating area is downstairs, a large homely room with white walls (and obligatory exposed brick feature), fireplaces, handsome wooden floors, scrubbed old school desks, comfy vintage armchairs and Chesterfields and free wifi – it's a lovely, welcoming space.

There's an extensive food service that includes breakfast/brunch (till noon on weekdays and 3.30pm at weekends), plus a good selection of cakes and pastries provided by a local artisan bakery (rich chocolate brownies, banana loaves, carrot cake, etc.). Brunch ranges from healthy options (granola, muesli, porridge, boiled eggs with soldiers) to the Full Monty (an upmarket version of bacon and eggs featuring prosciutto and Gruyere cheese, or Leyas' vegetarian version).

Leyas also host tasting mornings, when you can try a range of coffees, teas and hot chocolate (see website for info).

Leyas, 20 Camden High St, NW1 0JH (www. leyas.co.uk; Mornington Cres tube; Mon-Fri 7.30am-6pm, Sat-Sun 9am-6pm).

Long White Cloud

An attractive coffee shop, eatery and gallery on Hackney Road in Hoxton, Long White Cloud – the Maori name for New Zealand is Aotearoa or 'land of the long white cloud' – occupies a long white room furnished with vintage wooden tables and chairs, plants, flowers and art on the walls. However, it isn't the décor that attracts the crowds but the excellent coffee (Monmouth) and delicious food.

The friendly LWC offers a tasty free-range, locally sourced, all-day breakfast and brunch menu (see website), ranging from French toast with bacon, bananas and agave syrup to smoked salmon and scrambled eggs, corn fritter stack with avocado or bacon to mackerel with free-range scrambled eggs, and roasted garlic mushrooms on toast to the usual hearty full English (or full Kiwi) plus veggie option. In addition there's a simple evening menu served on weekdays, including all-you-can-eat pasta on Monday and Tuesday, pie on Wednesday, Mexican on Thursday and burgers on Friday. The café is licensed, too.

There's also live jazz with the nachos on Thursdays (until midnight) and changing art exhibitions (see website for information).

Long White Cloud, 151 Hackney Rd, E2 8JL (020-7033 4642; http://longwhitecloudhoxton. com; Hoxton rail; Mon-Wed, Fri 7am-8pm, Thu 7am-midnight, Sat-Sun 8am-6pm).

Maison d'être

A delightful little independent coffee house at Highbury Corner, Maison d'être was established in 2011 by Kim (baker extraordinaire) and Kosta (coffee geek). The cosy café – decked out with vintage furniture and crockery – is augmented by a lovely rear conservatory. In addition to super coffee from Square Mile, there's also quality loose-leaf tea from the Canton Tea Co, superb hot chocolate from the Kokoa Collection, juices and smoothies.

Maison uses local, seasonal and organic ingredients from some of London's finest suppliers, including Farm Direct (fresh produce), Paul Rhodes Bakery, E5 Bakehouse and Seven Seeded (bread

and Viennoiserie), while most cakes and other baked treats are made in-house. The all-day breakfast menu (till 4pm) features lighter treats such as homemade granola with Greek yoghurt or ricotta with figs and honey on sourdough, while lunch comprises soup, salads and terrific sandwiches: try the chorizo, kimchi and grilled cheddar on sourdough.

Weekend brunch (9am-4pm) includes such mouth-watering delights as French toast with banana, crispy pancetta and maple syrup, and crumpets with smoked salmon, avocado, beetroot pickle, mascarpone and pistachios. Add in good music, free wifi, newspapers and smiles, and you've found yourself a goldmine.

Maison d'être, 154 Canonbury Rd, N1 2UP (020-7226 4711; www.maisondetrecafe.co.uk; Highbury & Islington tube; Mon-Fri 7.30am-7pm, Sat-Sun 9am-6pm).

Monmouth Coffee

One of the pioneers of the first wave of coffee shops and roasters that have been brewing up a storm in London, Monmouth opened their first roast-and-retail outlet in Covent Garden's Monmouth Street (hence the name) in 1978. Roasting is now done in Maltby Street (Bermondsey), from where they supply coffee shops throughout the city, and they also have an outlet in Borough Market.

Monmouth's beans come from single farms, estates and cooperatives, with buyers travelling the world seeking out interesting varietals. They are equally fussy about their other ingredients, such as organic Jersey whole milk (from Jeff Bowles in Somerset) and organic whole cane sugar imported from Assukkar in Costa Rica.

Monmouth's cult shop in Covent Garden is a simple affair by today's standards, with snug tables in the back and a few benches outside. There's a tempting array of cakes and pastries – including lovely croissants and pain au chocolat – plus filled rolls and other goodies, but coffee is king here. You can buy coffee – whole beans or ground to your specification – in all three shops (or order by phone).

Monmouth Coffee, 27 Monmouth St, WC2H 9EU (020-7232 3010; www.monmouthcoffee.co.uk; Covent Gdn tube; Mon-Sat 8am-6.30pm, closed Sun).

New Row Coffee

A proper coffee shop in a quiet back street near Leicester Square, New Row is run by passionate coffee geeks. Their coffee is brewed to perfection using a V-60 pour-over and bursting with flavour – and not an Americano or decaf in sight (but do try the iced espresso).

Beans are sourced from Union Hand Roasted and the coffee is stupendous, as is the irresistible array of cakes and pastries – red velvet cake, Portuguese *pastel de nata*, fabulous croissants and huge cookies – and tasty savoury sandwiches. The only downside is the limited number of tables and seats inside – there's a bench outside – but then standing is good for you!

New Row Coffee, 24 New Row, WC2N 4LA (020-3583 6949; http://newrowcoffee.co.uk; Leicester Sq tube; Mon-Fri 7.30am-7pm, Sat-Sun 8.30am-7pm).

Notes

Now with five branches (others in Canary Wharf, King's Cross and Moorgate), Notes takes its coffee (and tea, sourced from Lalani) very seriously. It has had its own roastery since 2013 and has a dedicated brew bar showcasing a rotating menu of filter coffees.

Notes serves homemade food, including cakes and pastries, a range of salads, sandwiches, soups and tarts at lunchtimes, and cheese and meat boards and seasonal plates in the evenings – all washed down with reasonably-priced wines. It also sells coffee beans and coffee-making equipment, both in its shops and online.

Notes, 31 St Martin's Ln, WC2N 4ER (020-7240 0424; http://notes-uk.co.uk; Charing Cross tube/rail; Mon-Wed Fri 7.30am-9pm, Thu-Fri 7.30am-10pm, Sat 9am-10pm, Sun 10am-6pm).

Nude Espresso

This cool café on Soho Square is the second offering from Kiwi-owned Nude Espresso, whose Brick Lane coffee shop is the stuff of legend – the Nude team won Independent Café of the Year UK in 2010 and 2013 (awarded by the Café Society). The Soho outlet is sleek and modern, with a plush mezzanine level and alfresco tables

for sunny days. As well as brilliant brews, Nude sells a wide range of delicious food: fresh paninis, tasty sandwiches and creative salads, plus tempting cakes and pastries.

If you want to unleash your inner barista, they host coffee cupping (tasting) and training sessions at their East End roastery.

Nude Espresso, 19 Soho Sq, W1D 3QN (07712-899336, www.nudeespresso.com/cafes/soho-square; Tottenham Court Rd tube; Mon-Fri 7.30am-5pm, closed weekends).

Ozone

Ozone is a dedicated café and roastery with its origins in New Plymouth, New Zealand, which spread its wings to Shoreditch in 2012. Nowadays their superb, freshly-roasted coffee doesn't have to travel far as it's roasted and ground on-site.

The relaxed Antipodean-style café – with exposed brickwork, weathered tables, comfy booths and huge windows – is a lovely spot

to hang out and enjoy excellent coffee and homemade food. The Ozone menu ranges from cocktails to cakes – served from breakfast to dinner – all freshly prepared in-house.

Ozone Café & Roastery, 11 Leonard St, EC2A 4AQ (020-7490 1039; www.ozonecoffee.co.uk; Old St tube; Mon-Fri 7.30am-10pm, Sat-Sun 9am-5pm).

Prufrock Coffee

Prufrock's flagship café on buzzy Leather Lane is a shrine to coffee, founded by the legendary Gwilym Davies (pictured), 2009 UK and World Barista Champion – and no, he isn't from Down Under – he's a Yorkshireman. Davies is at the forefront

of coffee's 'third wave' – a movement to raise awareness of coffee as a hand-made product, focusing as much on provenance as wine-making does.

Prufrock has its own in-house bakery and offers a seasonal menu using produce from many of London's best producers. The bright and bustling café is also home to the London Barista Resource and Training Centre, one of the city's leading coffee schools, and sells coffee beans and coffee-making equipment.

Prufrock Coffee, 23-25 Leather Ln, EC1N 7TE (020-7242 0467; www.prufrockcoffee.com; Farringdon tube; Mon-Fri 8am-6pm, Sat-Sun 10am-5pm).

Rapha Cycle Club

Rapha are world leaders in cycling wear and accessories, and they're also rather serious about coffee. Thus the Rapha Cycle Club is both a cycle store and coffee shop (beans from Workshop). The café area occupies around half the floor space, with ample seating and ultra-friendly staff.

The creative menu consists of a range of hearty breakfast, lunch and snack options designed to prepare and replenish cyclists. A clever touch is the inclusion of dishes influenced by people and places from the world of cycling, e.g. the Paolo Bettini toasted sandwich: chicken breast, semi-dried tomatoes, watercress and olive tapenade. The café is licensed and you can watch live cycling action on screen.

Rapha Cycle Club, 85 Brewer St, W1F 9ZN (020-7494 9831; http://pages.rapha.cc/clubs/london; Piccadilly Circus; Mon-Fri 8am-8pm, Sat 8.30am-7.30pm, Sun 11am-6pm).

Reilly Rocket

Styling itself a motorcycle café, Reilly Rocket is a cool coffee shop in Dalston serving exceptional (Square Mile) coffee – plus a good range of teas from Waterloo – and splendid food inspired by the sunny cafés of Melbourne. The homely café has whitewashed brick walls, a mishmash of comfortable leather chairs and tables, memorabilia, art and plants. It's a long way from what most people would expect of a bikers' hangout – and the food is far from greasy spoon.

Reilly Rocket serves a changing menu of brilliant dishes using locally sourced and seasonal ingredients. Start the day with a healthy bowl of granola or porridge followed by a breakfast bap with smoked streaky bacon, chive and parmesan omelette with rocket and tomato relish, or poached eggs on sourdough. For lunch there are creative sandwiches (such as Ginger Pig sausage, red onion jam, crisp lettuce, mustard and mayo on toasted multigrain) and bagels (try the grilled halloumi with tomato, fresh lime and spicy tomato relish). There are also daily specials such as smoked BBQ pulled pork served on apple sourdough with red cabbage and walnut slaw. Excellent value and superior food – this place rocks!

Reilly Rocket, 507 Kingsland Rd, E8 4AU (020-7241 6363; www.reillyrocket.com; Dalston Junc rail; Mon-Fri 7.30am-5pm, Sat 9am-5pm, Sun 10am-5pm).

Reynolds

This is Reynolds' second branch – the first opened in 2007 on Eastcastle Street, W1 – serving superb coffee from Volcano and Union made on a Simonelli Aurelia machine (as used in the World Barista Championships) in a vintage-style café with mix-and-match furniture.

The food menu is fairly extensive, although portions are small – Reynolds' philosophy promotes grazing, i.e. eating little but often. There's a kitchen on-site but food is also bought in, such as organic breads, cakes and pastries from artisan bakers, including favourites such as chocolate brownies, banana bread and lemon drizzle cake. The interesting menu includes everything from salads and dips to wraps and rolls, sandwiches and baguettes to pies and tarts. Good things come in small packages!

Reynolds, 53 Charlotte St, W1T 4PA (020-7580 0730; www.letsgrazereynolds.co.uk; Goodge St tube; Mon-Fri 7.30am-5pm, closed weekends).

Roastery

A cosy artisan coffee mecca in Battersea/Clapham, the Roastery is, as the name suggests, both a roastery and a coffee shop. The welcoming Kiwi-owned café boasts attractive contemporary décor and plenty of seating inside, plus a few outside tables for those rare sunny mornings.

The excellent strong coffee (double shots are served as standard – no wussy lattes here) is complemented by a small food offering, which includes tasty filled bagels and a selection of cakes and pastries such as ANZAC and Afghan biscuits (made with cocoa and cornflakes). At weekends they serve all-day brunch including salmon and scrambled eggs, eggs Benedict, full English, veggie breakfast, French toast and more.

Roastery, 789 Wandsworth Rd, SW8 3JQ (020-7350 1961; Wandsworth Rd rail/Clapham Common tube; Mon-Fri 8am-5pm, Sat-Sun 9am-5pm).

Sacred

A New Zealand-style café founded by Tubbs Wanisgasekera and Matthew Clark, who wanted to bring their home café culture to Londoners, Sacred has grown into a small chain with the original in Ganton Street (just off Carnaby Street). It's a welcoming place set over two floors – think dark wood, comfortable sofas, poufs and cushions – with an alfresco seating area.

The house coffee is a typical NZ roast (organic and Fairtrade), mellow and aromatically complex with a full body, moderate acidity and nutty/earthy flavours. Sacred are also serious about their loose-leaf tea, imported from Sri Lanka and served in quirky teapots. There's also a wide range of soft drinks.

Food options include a light breakfast menu (muesli, bacon sandwich, filled bagels, scrambled eggs, grilled tomatoes, avocado on toast, etc.), sandwiches/paninis, cakes and pastries, plus hummus, cheese and antipasti platters in the evenings. It's also licensed and does a nice line in hot cocktails – try the berry sapphire (a blend of Sacred's signature red berry tea with Aperol and Bombay Sapphire gin, served in a vintage style teapot) or Irish dream (Sacred chai and Baileys topped with steamed milk dusted with cinnamon). Awesome!

Sacred, 13 Ganton St, W1F 9BL (020-7734 1415; http://sacredcafe.co.uk; Oxford Circus tube; Mon-Wed 7.30am-10pm, Thu-Fri 7.30am-11pm, Sat 9am-11pm, Sun 9.30am-10pm).

St David Coffee House

This charming, wisteria-clad café in Forest Hill is more like an eccentric aunt's front room than a coffee house, with walls lined with well-thumbed books (the café runs a book exchange) and work by local artists. The décor may be slightly kitsch but the folk who run St David are serious about their coffee (Square Mile), tea and delicious food,

much of it homemade or sourced from artisan producers. It's also licensed and serves craft beer,

There's a large communal table by the open window for sociable sipping, or grab one of the pavement tables on a sunny day. A local treasure.

St David Coffee House, 5 David's Rd, SE23 3EP (020-8291 6646; www.stdavidcoffeehouse. co.uk; Forest Hill rail; Tue 8am-5pm, Wed-Fri 8am-11pm, Sat 9am-11pm, Sun 10am-4pm, closed Mon).

Saint Espresso

Drinking coffee here might not quite be a holy experience, but it's certainly memorable. Saint Espresso is brought to you by the team behind Leyas (see page 97); dedicated coffee specialists, they use beans from various roasters and serve V60, Aeropress and cold brew coffee. They also offer an outstanding selection of premium teas (Lelani). The chic, beautifully-designed café – clean black lines, warm wood and copper accents – is relatively spacious, although short on seating.

The food choice includes toasties, cakes and pastries, e.g. croissants, sea-salt caramel brownies and muffins. Not a place for a hearty lunch, but a great venue for a heavenly brew.

Saint Espresso, Angel House, 26 Pentonville Rd, N1 9HJ (www.saintespresso.com; Angel tube; Mon-Fri 7.30am-6pm, Sat-Sun 9am-6pm).

Sharps Coffee Bar

Occupying the front half of a Fitzrovia barbers shop, Sharps Coffee Bar represents the second collaboration of coffee legends Rob Dunne and Victor Frankowski. From the street, the shop's branding features the barbers, although there's a board outside stating 'Dunne Frankowski Coffee Bar'.

The coffee bar, separated from the barbers shop by a wood and glass partition, is starkly decorated: white tiles, whitewashed walls and a wooden floor. It's dominated by a large counter and sparsely furnished with a few alfresco benches, a window-bar and a number of low tables and wooden benches. But you come here for coffee (and cuts), not comfort…

Various coffee options are offered – made with a rotating range of beans from high-class roasters (Square Mile, Workshop, etc.) – including espresso from the handsome Spirit Triplette machine and filter coffee

through an Aeropress or a more conventional filter machine. Dunne Frankowski also offers tasting menus, allowing you to compare different aspects of coffee, e.g. espresso and cappuccino.

There's a limited food and cake menu and the café also hosts regular food residencies from pop-up outfits – but it's the coffee that's the draw here. And where else can you get your beard trimmed while sipping an espresso?

Sharps Coffee Bar, 9 Windmill St, W1T 2JF (020-7636 8688; http://dunnefrankowski. com/2014/sharps-coffee-bar-by-dunnefrankowski; Goodge St tube; Mon, Fri 10am-7pm, Tue-Thu 10am-8pm, Sat 10am-6pm, Sun 11am-6pm).

Store Street Espresso

Located in the heart of Uni-land in Bloomsbury (close to the British Museum), Store Street Espresso is a handsome, minimalist coffee shop. The bright, long room – white walls with ever-changing art, wooden floor, hanging lamps, large windows and an attractive skylight at the rear – has lots

of seating, including some outside. There are small tables and niches where you can settle down to surf the web (power points in the rear), although it gets crowded at peak times.

The superb house blend is from Square Mile (Red Brick), supplemented by a changing roster of guest beans. The excellent food is mostly made in-house and includes a light breakfast menu supplemented by a daily brunch (until 3pm) which includes the likes of grilled halloumi, poached eggs, avocado and roasted tomatoes on courgette and carrot fritters, and *sabich*, an Israeli sandwich featuring grilled aubergine, boiled eggs, with hummus, tahini and mango pickle stuffed into warm pitta bread.

There's also an enticing selection of homemade cakes (delicious brownies, banana bread, etc.), pastries and sandwiches on the counter. Good value, friendly service, nice music, free wifi, newspapers and books – a class act.

Store Street Espresso, 40 Store St, WC1E 7DB (www.storestespresso.co.uk; Goodge St tube; Mon-Fri 7.30am-7pm, Sat 9am-6pm, Sun 10am-5pm).

TAP Coffee

TAP Coffee (formerly Tapped & Packed) has three outlets, the original Fitzrovia café, plus Tottenham Court Road and Wardour Street (featured here), all identified by an outsize street number and old-fashioned grocer's bike outside. The attractive long room has skylights running almost its entire length, with dark wood benches, stools, tables and flooring.

TAP offers an impressive variety of excellent coffee – made with their own beans roasted in-house – and different brewing methods, including siphon, pour-over, Aeropress and cafetière. There's a good selection of cakes and pastries, accompanied by sandwiches and salads at lunchtime. Friendly, relaxing and satisfying.

Tap Coffee, 193 Wardour St, W1F 8ZF (020-7580 2163; www.tapcoffee.co.uk; Tottenham Court Rd tube; Mon-Fri 8am-7pm, Sat 10am-6pm, Sun 11am-6pm).

Taylor Street Baristas

Founded in 2006 by Aussie siblings Nick, Andrew and Laura Tolley, Taylor Street now has eight outlets in the city, so it goes without saying that their coffee (Union) is superb. The Bank branch (their largest, featured here) has recently had a makeover and is now a lovely bright space full of nice details, from the unique floor to the custom-made shelves.

There's a take-away section, a sit-in area and a brew bar dedicated to hand-brewed coffee. The seasonal food menu includes lush avocado toast, banana bread with homemade 'Nutella', Vegemite and cheese sourdough muffins, tasty sandwiches and creative salads. There's free wifi and plenty of power sockets, too.

Taylor St Baristas, 125 Old Broad St, EC2N 1AR (020-7256 8665; www.taylor-st.com; Bank tube; Mon-Fri 7am-6pm, closed weekends).

Timberyard

Timberyard occupies a huge 'versatile lifestyle space' over two floors in Old Street, with eclectic furnishings and counters equipped with iPads for customers' use. Coffee is the main draw, made with Has Bean's signature Jabberwocky blend, although the specialist teas also score highly. There's always a good range of baked goods, sandwiches and salads, plus granola and porridge for breakfast – and it's licensed.

Timberyard (TY for short) bills itself as a place to work and play; there's good wifi, plenty of sockets and no-one will complain if you linger over your drink. There's another branch in Covent Garden.

Timberyard, 61-67 Old St, EC1V 9HW (020-3217 2009; http://tyuk.com; Old St/Barbican tube; Mon-Fri 8am-8pm, Sat-Sun 10am-6pm).

Tinto Coffee

Owned by Paul, a friendly Colombian, Tinto Coffee in Fulham (close to Bishop's Park and Fulham Palace) is a great place to chill out with a newspaper and a coffee. Cosy, peaceful and refreshingly untrendy, this friendly neighbourhood café has the bonus of a heated outdoor seating area.

Tinto serves its own blend of Fairtrade coffee (Colombian naturally) and a wide range of fresh food, including filled bagels, toasties, quiche, baguettes and muffins, plus a good selection of freshly-baked cakes and pastries (croissants, polenta cake, gluten-free chocolate brownies). There's also free wifi, a large iMac, newspapers and a small library. You'll never want to leave…

Tinto Coffee, 411 Fulham Palace Court Rd, SW6 6SX (020-7731 8232; Putney Br tube; daily 7am-9pm).

Tomtom Coffee House

A quirky little establishment in Belgravia, Tomtom Coffee House (named after co-owner Tom Assheton) is exactly that: an old-fashioned traditional coffee house. There's no wifi but there is convivial company, with

a large communal table and plenty of alfresco seating.

Tomtom sources beans from around the globe, which are roasted in-house and available as individual filter drinks. Delicious food is served all day, from breakfast boiled eggs to lunchtime pasties and pies and early evening nibbles in summer. You can choose from a range of freshly-baked cakes, along with homemade Poilâne toasties. Tomtom is licensed and sells coffee beans for home consumption.

Tomtom Coffee House, 114 Ebury St, SW1W 9QD (020-7730 1771; www.tomtom.co.uk; Sloane Sq/Victoria tube; Mon-Fri 8am-6pm, Sat-Sun 9am-6pm).

Trade

An independent coffee shop and sandwich bar in busy Spitalfields, Trade occupies a former menswear shop that's been given a sympathetic makeover. It's now a striking space with exposed brickwork, lots of attractive dark wood, a huge service counter, bespoke tables and chairs, copper highlights, bare bulbs and a lovely decked terrace area.

It offers speciality coffees, quality teas and homemade food, including scrummy cakes, cookies and muffins, interesting salads and sandwiches made with artisan breads. Ingredients and produce are sourced from artisan producers and nearby Spitalfields Market, while out back there's a small smokery where pastrami and other deli meats are produced.

Trade, 47 Commercial St, E1 6BD (020-3490 1880; www.trade-made.co.uk; Aldgate East tube; Mon-Fri 7.30am-5pm, Sat-Sun 10am-5pm).

Vagabond

Vagabond first set up shop in Stroud Green in 2011 and has since opened another two branches, in Holloway Road and Whitechapel High Street. The original is a labour of coffee-geek love, made from reclaimed wood and discarded materials. It's a bit ramshackle and scruffy, but welcoming and friendly – somewhere a true vagabond may feel at home – with coffee-themed photos on the walls and a nice outdoor seating area.

The coffee (Has Been and Union) is predictably excellent and changes regularly, as does the food menu of homemade cakes (apple, carrot or banana cake made with wholemeal flour), pastries and sandwiches, soup of the day and omelettes.

Vagabond, Charter Court, Stroud Green Rd, N4 3SG (020-8616 4514; www.vagabond.london; Crouch Hill rail; daily 7am-7pm).

Venetia's

A small family-friendly coffee shop, Venetia's has been a fixture on Chatsworth Road in Clapton since 2007 and is a local hub for gossip, coffee and good food. The cosy interior – simply designed with wooden floors, white wood-panelled walls and exposed brick – may be on the small side, but there's also a spacious (covered and heated) terrace at the back and a few tables out front in good weather.

Venetia's serves excellent coffee (Darlingtons) and tea (Tea Pigs), and artisan food from the likes of the Crazy Baker, Coombe Farm and Galeta Cookie Heaven. Food includes delicious homemade cakes, tasty sandwiches (made with artisan bread), salads, soups and stews. There's also free wifi.

Venetia's, 55 Chatsworth Rd, E5 0LH (020-8986 1642; www.venetias.co.uk; Homerton rail; daily 8am-6pm).

Volcano Coffee House

As any coffee aficionado will know, Volcano is a leading Kiwi-owned coffee roaster; but you may not know that Volcano has a café next door to its roastery in West Norwood, south London. The stylish coffee shop – a hidden jewel at the heart of Parkhall Trading Estate – occupies a huge white industrial (yet serene) space in a grand '30s warehouse building.

The café offers a wide range of Volcano's superb coffee (the aromas are intoxicating) made with their lovely La Marzocco Linea machine, accompanied by an array of tasty looking cakes, pastries, salads and sandwiches. And you can buy coffee beans to brew at home.

Volcano Coffee House, Unit F01, Parkhall Trading Estate, 40 Martell Rd, SE21 8EN (020-8670 8927; http://volcanocoffeeworks.com; West Norwood rail; Mon-Fri 8am-4pm, Sat 9am-1pm, closed Sun).

The Watch House

Styling itself 'a luxury artisan coffee house', the Watch House is a tiny café housed in a striking octagonal building on Bermondsey Street. The 19th-century Watch House building was built to house the guards who protected the graves of St Mary Magdalen church from body-snatchers. It's been beautifully renovated with its original rustic stone walls enhanced by colourful art (for sale) and black-and-white tiled floors.

The team is passionate about its coffee, made with Fairtrade premium espresso blends exclusively roasted for the Watch House by Ozone. Food consists of a tempting selection of breakfast/brunch dishes, cakes and pastries, and homemade sandwiches, baguettes, salads and soups.

The Watch House, 193 Bermondsey St, SE1 3UW (020-7407 5431, www.watchhousecoffee.com; Borough tube; Mon-Fri 7am-6pm, Sat 8am-6pm, Sun 9am-6pm).

Wild & Wood Coffee

Voted 'London Coffee Shop of the Year 2014' by London Lifestyle Awards, bijou Wild & Wood is entirely furnished with antique church furniture, giving it a tranquil air. A '50s soundtrack adds to the atmosphere and there's also alfresco seating if you prefer.

Serving superb Monmouth coffee (the blend changes weekly), with food from Clarke's of Kensington and Cocomaya artfully displayed in the window and fresh juices from Devon, it's a top place to chill. There's a good selection of cakes and pastries (lovely cheesecake and croissants), excellent sandwiches quiche, frittata and more. Good value, too.

Wild & Wood Coffee, 47 London Wall, EC2M 5TE (07525-155957; http://wildandwoodcoffee. co.uk; Moorgate tube; Mon-Fri 7am-5pm, Sat 10am-3pm, closed Sun).

Wired Co.

Just around the corner from West Hampstead tube station you'll find Wired Co., one of the area's best speciality coffee shops. The small relaxing café serves outstanding Climpson coffee, with a large board detailing the origins and flavours of the beans on offer (in simple non-geek speak).

Beyond the coffee the food on offer is fairly basic and includes toast, toasted banana bread (recommended), granola (with yogurt, berries and honey) and filled croissants, plus toasties, soup and focaccia sandwiches. There's also a selection of cakes and pastries from Babycakes of Kensal Green. Not a place for a hearty lunch, but it's the coffee that's the main attraction.

Wired Co., 194 Broadhurst Gdns, NW6 3AY (020-7372 4400/07444-421087; W Hampstead tube; Mon-Fri 7.30am-5pm, Sat-Sun 9am-5pm).

Workshop Coffee Co.

This highly regarded coffee roaster opened its first café on Clerkenwell Road in 2011 (there are now four branches, including the Fitzrovia Coffee Bar on page 90) and has been scooping up awards ever since, including a 'Best Independent Café' at

the Café Society Awards. Since then it has evolved into a thriving destination, not just for coffee lovers but also for foodies, adding breakfast, lunch, dinner and weekend brunch to its repertoire. The décor is contemporary industrial chic, light and spacious with high ceilings, bare floorboards and exposed brick and pipes.

It's a cool all-day dining spot serving innovative breakfasts – try the spiced pear and pistachio bread with lime cream cheese,

maple syrup and bacon – delicious brunches and lunches (sourdough 'brat' with bacon, rocket, avocado and tomato) and creative dinners. The upstairs dining room serves a fusion menu of small and large plates and grazing dishes, happily combining Asian and Mediterranean flavours with a dash of Middle Eastern magic. Dishes may include Dexter burger; smoked haddock fish cake; pork belly; grilled quail; potato, leek and gruyere tortilla; and much more. Scrumptious food and coffee, friendly service and a super atmosphere. Fantastic!

Workshop Coffee Co., 27 Clerkenwell Rd, EC1M 5RN (020-7253 5754; www.workshopcoffee. com; Farringdon tube; Mon 7.30am-6pm, Tue-Fri 7.30am-10pm, Sat-Sun 8am-6pm).

The Wren

The Wren is a non-profit coffee bar boasting one of the City's best locations in St Nicholas Cole Abbey (still in use), a Grade I listed church between St Paul's Cathedral and the Thames with a history dating back to the 12th century. Rebuilt by Sir Christopher Wren (hence the name) and again after

the Second World War, the abbey's soaring stone columns and lovely stained glass windows provide a tranquil oasis in the City, with plenty of seating in the spacious and elegant interior (there's a terrace, too).

In addition to seriously good coffee from Workshop – with the seasonal Cult of Done blend on espresso and rotating single origin beans on the V60 filter – there's fine tea (Brew Tea Co.) and a range of soft drinks. Wren does delicious breakfasts – sourdough toast, granola, pastries, etc. – plus sandwiches, quiches, salads and soups (from Norman Loves in Walthamstow).

Baked goods are from the likes of Sally Clarke's bakery in Kensington and the Candlestick Bakery, and include vanilla and strawberry friands, almond and dark chocolate cake and scrumptious cupcakes. Sir Christopher would approve!

The Wren, St Nicholas Cole Abbey, 114 Queen Victoria St, EC4V 4BJ (www.thewrencoffee. com; Mansion House/St Paul's tube; Mon-Fri 7am-5pm, closed weekends).

3. Tearooms

The British get through over 165 million cups of tea a day – that's around two teas to every coffee – a liquid love affair stretching back more than 300 years. Initially enjoyed only by the upper classes, by the late 19th century tearooms were all the rage in London and quickly become *the* place for meeting friends and sharing gossip, and were also one of the few respectable venues where women could meet without a chaperone.

Today, tearooms serve high-quality loose-leaf teas from every corner of the globe – an amazing 1,500 varieties are produced – including deep and fragrant blacks, herbal and infused reds, greens and oolongs from China and Japan, and the finest whites. Tearooms also offer a wealth of home-made treats, including bespoke cakes, Viennoiserie, freshly-baked scones and tempting savoury dishes.

This chapter features around 30 of London's best tearooms where you're guaranteed the perfect cuppa, irresistible cakes and pastries, a scrumptious traditional afternoon tea – and often a delicious lunch, too.

Tea was made fashionable by Charles II's wife, Queen Catherine – before which it was mainly drunk by men in coffee houses – and as demand grew, the powerful East India Company flooded the domestic market with tea. By 1750, it had replaced coffee as Britain's favourite drink – and the rest is history!

Amanzi

Originally founded in the US but now British-based and owned, Amanzi is a temple to tea located in the heart of Marylebone. Its chic exterior is complemented by a smart minimalist interior set over two floors, including a spacious tea house downstairs. Amanzi is passionate about tea and dedicated to creating unique drinks and blends. It offers an amazing 150 kinds of premium loose-leaf tea, plus a tea bar with baristas, tea tastings and tea-making equipment.

If you're after a pot of tea, you have over 40 to choose from on Amanzi's signature tea wall, which is divided into black, white, rooibos, beneficial and herbal tisane teas. There's also chai (spiced tea), matcha lattes, tea-based frappés, tea-based smoothies, iced tea lemonades, a range of bubble teas and virgin tea-based cocktails such as 'lychee mar-tea-ni'. For those less

adventurous there's English breakfast, Earl Grey and even coffee on the menu.

To accompany your tea, tuck into an assortment of cakes and pastries from Cocomaya (see page 145) – including dairy- and gluten-free options – such as cinnamon buns and mini croissants laced with the Middle Eastern herb and spice blend za'atar, plus a range of savouries, e.g. goat's cheese tarts. A tea-aholic's paradise.

Amanzi, 24 New Cavendish St, W1G 8TX (020-7935 5510, www.amanzitea.co.uk; Bond St tube; Mon-Fri 7.30am-7pm, Sat 10am-7pm, Sun 10am-6pm).

Bea's of Bloomsbury

This vintage-sounding tearoom opened in 2008 and was soon established as one of London's best. Located in a former bank, Bea's is a cosy place with shabby-chic décor and an open-plan pastry kitchen so you can watch the staff conjuring up brownies, cookies, a vast range of cupcakes, loaf cakes, marshmallows, meringues and much

more. The Bloomsbury shop supplies Bea's branches in Farringdon and St Paul's. Most famous for its heavenly cakes and pastries, Bea's also dishes up superb savoury food, including homemade frittatas, filled focaccia loaves, marinated chicken thighs, and spinach and ricotta rolls.

Although it serves tea and cake at any time, Bea's is best-known for its afternoon tea: you can tuck into freshly-baked scones with Cornish clotted cream and jam, fruity marshmallows, assorted brownies, mini savoury brioche buns and baguettes, accompanied by a wide selection of loose-leaf teas from the Jing Tea Company – along with an optional glass of champagne. Note that bookings are necessary for afternoon tea (daily, 11.30am-7pm). Gluten-free afternoon tea is available too.

Bea's also design and bake cakes for special occasions, including cakes.

Bea's of Bloomsbury, 44 Theobalds Rd, WC1X 8NW (020-7242 8330; www.beasofbloomsbury. com/pages/bloomsbury-1; Chancery Ln tube; Mon-Fri 7.30am-7pm, Sat-Sun 10am-7pm).

Belle Epoque Patisserie

Belle Epoque is a traditional French patisserie, bakery and chocolatier – widely recognised as one of the best pastry-makers in London – with a lovely tea room. Secreted away on Newington Green, the shop was opened in 2002 and offers bespoke cakes, pastel-hued macarons, mouth-watering Viennoiseries, fluffy quiches, traditional French bread and much more,

accompanied by a range of teas (and coffee).

At the rear of the shop, the attractive tearoom is decorated in Provençal style, while on sunny days you can enjoy the secluded garden. There's a second branch on Upper Street in Islington.

Belle Epoque Patisserie, 37 Newington Grn, N16 9PR (020-7249 2222; http://belleepoque. co.uk; Canonbury rail; Mon-Wed 8am-6pm, Thu-Fri 8am-7pm, Sat 9am-7pm, Sun 9am-6pm).

Candella Tea Room

Located on Kensington Church Street, the Candella Tea Room offers around 100 organic loose-leaf teas from every corner of the globe including deep and fragrant blacks, herbal and infused reds, rooibos from South Africa, greens and oolongs from China and Japan, and the finest whites. They also offer a huge range of homemade artisan cakes and tortes, cream teas and sandwiches, plus breakfast treats and gourmet lunches.

The cosy, romantic interior has French Baroque accents creating the atmosphere of an enchanted hideaway, with pastel frescoes on the walls and ceiling casting a warm glow. It's a lovely spot for a cuppa with someone special.

Candella Tea Room, 34 Kensington Church St, W8 4HA (020-7937 4161; www.candellatearoom. co.uk; High St Kensington tube; daily 9am-7pm).

Le Chandelier

A tea house and licensed café-restaurant on Lordship Lane in trendy East Dulwich, Le Chandelier offers over 30 teas (by Jing) sourced from small family-owned suppliers. The beautiful *salon de thé*, a fusion of English and French/Moroccan décor, is decorated with antique chandeliers (naturally!), mirrors and plush armchairs. There's also an alfresco seating area out front.

You can choose from a wide selection of inviting cakes and pastries including cupcakes, brownies, meringues, cheesecake, Viennoiserie and scones, made either in-house or by local artisan bakers. There's also a breakfast menu, afternoon tea (served from 3-6pm), a Moroccan inspired lunch and dinner menu, plus tea-infused cocktails.

Le Chandelier, 161 Lordship Ln, SE22 8HX (020-8299 3344; www.lechandelier.co.uk; E/N Dulwich rail; Sun-Wed 9.30am-6pm, Thu-Sat 9.30am-10pm).

Drink Shop & Do

A café-meets-craft-workshop in the heart of King's Cross, Drink Shop & Do is a kitsch café by day, bar/club by night. It isn't an obvious choice as a tea room, but offers an excellent selection of some 30 teas – including seven kinds of green tea – and afternoon tea (with an optional Bellini or glass of bubbly). DS&D also sells a serious range of sandwiches and cakes, including vegan and gluten-free options.

For crafty folk they run classes ranging from floral headband-making to vintage make-up sessions, and you can also take home a retro tea-set or furniture (almost everything is for sale). Morphs into a bar cum dance club in the evenings!

Drink Shop & Do, 9 Caledonian Rd, N1 9DX (020-7278 4335; www.drinkshopdo.com; King's Cross/St Pancras tube; Mon-Thu 10.30am-midnight, Fri-Sat 10.30am-2am, Sun 10.30am-8pm).

Emporium Tea Rooms

A nostalgic vintage tea room, Emporium also serves breakfast and lunch. Part of Dimensions Community Enterprises, it's operated as a social enterprise working with pupils from TreeHouse School. In addition to serving a wide range of teas from W. Martyn and Monmouth coffee, Emporium does a traditional afternoon tea and party packages for both children and adults. The cake selection changes daily and includes freshly-baked scones with clotted cream and homemade jam, fruity flapjacks and cupcakes.

A 'fancy goods' gift shop offers a unique selection of vintage and handmade items, preserves and made-to-order artwork. Emporium also offers various classes for adults and children.

Emporium Tea Rooms, 818 High Rd, N12 9QY (020-3302 8050; www.emporiumtearooms. co.uk; W Finchley tube; Mon-Sat 9-6, closed Sun).

The Garden Café

Hidden away in the backstreets of Mayfair, the Garden Café in elevated Brown Hart Gardens (built in 1906 above the old Duke Street electricity substation) is a delightful peaceful oasis just a few steps from chaotic Oxford Street. Surrounded by open space and modern planting, this minimalist café – huge windows, polished stone floors, white furniture and solid wooden trestles – although not strictly a tearoom is a lovely spot to enjoy a cuppa, particularly on a sunny day when the glazed doors are thrown open.

The Garden Café serves a range of teas, coffee, freshly-baked cakes and pastries, and a selection of salads and sandwiches.

The Garden Café. Brown Hart Gardens, Duke St, W1K 6TD (020-7493 9995; www.benugo. com/public-spaces/the-garden-cafe; Bond St tube; Mon-Fri 8am–5pm, Sat 9am–5pm, Sun 10am–5pm).

High Tea of Highgate

High Tea of Highgate is a charming olde-worlde tea room with a pink façade, striped black and white awning, bunting and chandeliers made from vintage teacups. Its tea – loose-leaf and blended in-house – is served in proper china teacups with milk in a cow creamer.

Owner Georgina Worthington, along with her team of delightful tea ladies and tea boys, creates traditional scrumptious treats such as lemon drizzle cake, scones, Victoria sponge, carrot cake, chocolate butter-cream sponge, lavender cake and wheat-free, almond-heavy, chocolate orange cake. The specially blended loose-leaf teas include the usual suspects plus more exotic varieties such as almond (infused with almond pieces and essential oil), lavender and rosemary, Russian caravan (a blend of black teas with a hint of smokiness) and Miss Worthington's Rose (Rose Congou, a black tea scented with rose petals). There's no set afternoon tea menu, but you can put together your own (apart from sandwiches) from the delicious range of cakes and scones.

High Tea is best savoured at your leisure. It's a charming destination for afternoon tea (and excellent morning coffee) which balances nostalgia with crisp modern style.

High Tea of Highgate, 50 Highgate High St, N6 5HX (020-8348 3162, www.highteaofhighgate. com, Highgate tube, Tue-Sat 10am-5.30pm, Sun 11am-5.30pm, closed Mon).

Kusmi Tea

Founded in St Petersburg in 1867 by Pavel Michailovitch Kousmichoff and relocated to Paris after the Russian Revolution, Kusmi has a stellar reputation for its high quality teas. The British subsidiary was opened in 1907 at a time when London was the capital of the tea trade, and it's still a mecca for lovers of the leaf.

This intoxicating shop in Marylebone – stacked to the rafters with Kusmi's distinctive tins and packets – has a small tea room at the rear where you can taste teas (guided by an expert) and enjoy a selection of delicious cakes and eclairs. Not cheap, but what price a taste of heaven?

Kusmi Tea, 15 Marylebone High St, W1U 4NU (020-7487 4245; http://uk.kusmitea.com; Baker/ Bond St tube; Mon-Sat 10am-8pm, Sun 10am-6pm).

Ladurée Tearoom

Parisian tearoom Ladurée (est. 1862) is internationally renowned, especially for its scrumptious macarons. The London flagship of this iconic chain, situated on the ground floor of Harrods, comprises a collection of individually designed salons with velvet chairs and sumptuous décor – although in warm weather the most popular tables are outside on the terrace.

Ladurée may be most famous for its macarons, *mille-feuilles* and *tartes*, but the enticing lunch menu encompasses a selection of stylish dishes such as smoked salmon éclair and summer truffle omelette, plus an array of club sandwiches. The tearooms' pièce de résistance is the *l'heure du thé* (afternoon tea), which promises an impressive selection of finger sandwiches, mini Viennoiseries and irresistible mini pastries. *Magnifique!*

Ladurée, Harrods Ground Floor, 87-135 Brompton Rd, SW1X 7XL (020-3155 0111; www. harrods.com/content/the-store/restaurants/ ladurée; Knightsbridge tube; Mon-Sat 9am to 10pm, Sun 11am-6pm).

Lady Dinah's Cat Emporium

Lady Dinah's Cat Emporium in Shoreditch is London's first cat café, an idea which first took hold in Japan – there are some 40 cat cafés in Tokyo alone. Here you can eat and drink surrounded by (rescued) cats. It may seem like a gimmick or novelty, but the café attracted £100,000 in crowd-funding donations and took 7,000 bookings in its first 24 hours, becoming a phenomenon on social media.

Owned and run by Lauren Pears, Lady Dinah's is a real English tearoom, with a proper coffee-making area where baristas and staff serve afternoon tea in bone china with scones and clotted cream. Downstairs there's a jumble of mismatched sofas and chairs alongside china display cabinets and an assortment of tables, while cat toys and beds adorn the seats and floors, along with a clowder of contented cats. It feels like a café that just happens to be full of cats, rather than a cat's home that serves refreshments.

Walk-in customers can be accommodated, but if you're seeking afternoon tea or high tea you should book well in advance, particularly for weekends. There's a £6 cover charge which helps care for the cats and maintain the café for them.

Lady Dinah's Cat Emporium, 152-154 Bethnal Green Rd, E2 6DG (020-7729 0953; http://ladydinahs.com; Shoreditch High St tube; Mon-Tue, Fri-Sun 10am-5pm, closed Wed).

Lanka

Run by French cuisine chef Masayuki Hara (born in Japan), Lanka specialises in stunning cakes and pastries – the best of British, French and Japanese patisserie – and pure Ceylon/Sri Lankan teas from Euphorium. Recently relocated from Primrose Hill, the charming little shop has a lovely display counter, whitewashed walls and a tiny café area.

To accompany the excellent black teas and scented infusions, there's a wide selection of exquisite patisseries including tea-infused delights such as fragrant jasmine crème brûlée and green tea chocolate cake, plus traditional French pastries (strawberry *mille-feuille* with petit choux coated with raspberry fondant), gluten-free macarons, and Lanka's famous bread and butter pudding with mixed berries. Marvellous!

Lanka, 9 Goldhurst Terrace, NW6 3HX (020-7625 3366; www.lanka-uk.com; Finchley Rd rail/Swiss Cottage tube; Mon-Sat 10.30am-6.30pm, Sun 11am-5pm).

London Review Cake Shop

Located in one of London's most distinctive independent bookshops– a stone's throw from the British Museum in Bloomsbury – the London Review Cake Shop is a modern literary tea house.

In addition to a wide catalogue of fine loose-leaf teas from Jing and Postcard Teas, there's a library of gorgeous cakes such as gluten-free rose and pistachio cake, toffee macadamia-nut cheesecake, and rich chocolate and Guinness cake. Blackboards scattered around the shop offer clever tea pairings, specials and tea-related quotes. There's also a seasonally-inspired menu of savoury dishes, including soups, quiches, salads and hot dishes, plus a selection of *tartines* and sandwiches on artisanal breads.

London Review Cake Shop, 14 Bury Pl, WC1A 2JL (020-7269 9045; www. londonreviewbookshop.co.uk/cake-shop; Holborn tube; Mon-Sat 10am-6.30pm, closed Sun).

Maison Bertaux

Treat yourself to a cup of tea and a scrumptious cake at charming Maison Bertaux, an eccentric Soho landmark since 1871. It's an endearingly quirky patisserie/tearoom with a bijou downstairs room scattered with half a dozen mismatched tables and chairs, flowers and an old piano adorned with eclectic artworks (for sale). There's also a room upstairs, although weather permitting most habitués prefer to cram onto the pavement tables outside.

London's oldest patisserie and still one of the best, it has a lovely old-fashioned vibe, unpretentious and relaxed, if a bit run-down, with a stellar reputation for its freshly-baked Viennoiseries, croissants, croques and pastries. A Soho institution.

Maison Bertaux, 28 Greek St, W1D 5DQ (020-7437 6007; www.maisonbertaux.com; Leicester Sq tube; Mon-Sat 8.30am-11pm, Sun 9.30am-8pm).

The Muffin Man

A cosy old-fashioned English teashop in the heart of Kensington, the Muffin Man is a welcome retreat in this busy part of town. It offers a small variety of teas – they are also importers and vendors of loose-leaf teas – plus coffee and a wide range of irresistible cakes and pastries. Try the Queen Mother's Cake or passion carrot cake.

It's a great place for breakfast serving everything from a full English to muesli, toast and croissants. There's also a light lunch menu offering salads, soups, quiche, sandwiches and more. Afternoon tea comes with a choice of muffins (what else!), teacakes, sandwiches, scones, cakes and crumpets. Prices are reasonable, particularly for Kensington.

The Muffin Man, 12 Wrights Ln, W8 6TA (020-7937 6652; http://themuffinmankensington.co.uk; High St Kensington; Mon-Sat 8am-8pm, Sun 9am-8pm).

Orange Pekoe

A tea treasure house established in 2006, Orange Pekoe – the name describes a fine, large leaf tea of the highest quality – offers loose-leaf teas in their purest form, with owners Marianna and Achilleas

travelling far and wide to seek out the finest handpicked tea in the world. The tearoom is one London's best – its motto is 'for the art, the philosophy and the love of tea' – and a member of the Tea Council's prestigious Tea Guild, from whom it has received many awards of excellence since 2008.

Orange Pekoe offers everything from breakfast to lunch and afternoon tea, with a selection of freshly cut finger sandwiches, hot crumpets, fruit bread, cakes and pastries. Afternoon tea ranges from an informal all-day scones-and-cream tea to a more traditional tea (served from 2-5pm) including sandwiches, cake and a glass of fizz if desired.

All Orange Pekoe's teas (some 60 loose-leaf and flower teas) can be purchased in beautiful tea caddies or refill pouches. There's a trained tea sommelier on hand who can advise you on your choice and you're encouraged to open the caddies, smell the teas and admire the beautiful leaves.

Orange Pekoe, 3 White Hart Ln, SW13 0PX (020-8876 6070, www.orangepekoeteas.com, Barnes Br rail; Mon-Fri 7.30am-5pm, Sat-Sun 9am-5pm).

Peggy Porschen's Parlour

A leading bespoke cake company in Ebury Street, Belgravia, Peggy Porschen is one of London's most celebrated bakers and confectioners. Peggy's client list includes Madonna, Elton John and Damien Hirst – she really is cake-maker to the stars. The lovely parlour is reminiscent of one of Peggy's gorgeous creations: the exterior is candy-floss pink with large Georgian windows and a terrace, while inside are sugary hues, cream furniture and porcelain tableware.

The Parlour offers a range of scrumptious freshly-baked cakes and pastries (cupcakes, cookies, layer cakes, fruit cake, muffins, etc.) accompanied by a selection of house-blend teas or – if you're on a celebrity budget – a glass of pink champagne.

Peggy Porschen, 116 Ebury St, SW1W 9QQ (020-7730 1316, www.peggyporschen.com; Sloane Sq tube; daily 10am-6pm).

Pembroke Lodge Tea Rooms

A visit to Richmond Park wouldn't be complete without having tea (or high tea) at handsome Pembroke Lodge Tea Rooms, located in a magnificent 18th-century Georgian mansion with 11 acres of landscaped grounds. The lodge has been lovingly restored in recent years and now serves as a wedding venue and tea room.

It's the perfect spot to indulge in tea and cake on a sunny day on the expansive terrace. The tearooms also offer a variety of sandwiches and snacks, plus a changing lunch menu (choice of meat, fish and vegetarian dishes), all reasonable priced. However, the lodge – and its magnificent panorama – is the real star.

Pembroke Lodge Tea Rooms, Richmond Park, Richmond, TW10 5HX (020-8940 8207; www.pembroke-lodge.co.uk/the-tea-rooms; Richmond rail/tube; daily 9am-5.30 or 30 minutes before dusk in winter).

Piacha

A tea bar and shop in Upper Street with a fresh take on tea drinking, Piacha is all about interesting blends and skilfully brewed tea, accompanied by mellow jazz while relaxing in a comfy (orange!) armchair. Founded by Pia – hence the name, which also means 'drinking tea' – a tea enthusiast ex-lawyer with a background in technology and a passion for food, design and healthy

lifestyle. She created Piacha to provide tea lovers with some much needed pampering in the form of original blends, big mugs of full-flavoured tea, a fast takeaway service and an atmospheric tea bar.

Some 25 teas and blends are on offer – black, green, oolong, herbal, rooibos and hibiscus teas – which can be enjoyed in the tea bar where there's a never-ending tasting

session taking place. The teas are based on quality whole-leaf tea from select artisan producers blended with herbs, flowers, fruit and spices, to produce a range where each tea is an experience.

To accompany your brew there's a selection of cakes, pastries and tea-infused sandwiches – and cooling tea smoothies. A refreshing change from Islington's numerous coffee shops.

Piacha, 280 Upper St, N1 2TZ (020-7354 8365; www.piacha.co.uk; Essex Rd rail; Mon-Fri 9am-9pm, Sat-Sun 10am-9pm).

The Tea Box

Jemma Swallow's charming Tea Box was established in 2007 as an antidote to the plethora of coffee shops that had sprung up in the Richmond area (although it does serve Monmouth coffee). The homely 'colonial boutique-style' room, festooned with weighty chandeliers and furnished with an eclectic collection of antique-style furniture, offers comfortable seating and cosy corners.

The Tea Box is serious about its beverages and offers one of London's largest selections of loose-leaf tea; a whole wall is devoted to decorative tea canisters filled with prime pickings from the world's most famous tea plantations. There are over 60 teas and blends, including traditional favourites, fruity infusions such as blackcurrant and hibiscus, green tea scented with jasmine, tipsy tea cocktails, Moroccan mint tea, chai latte and the exotic sounding Ms Saigon.

High or afternoon tea (with an optional glass of champagne) includes a choice of sandwiches, a dozen varieties of scone and an abundance of scrumptious cakes (including gluten-free options), not forgetting the wide choice of teas. In the evening there's regular entertainment such as jazz and swing sessions, comedy, storytelling, poetry and more. A box of delights!

The Tea Box, 7 Paradise Rd, TW9 1RX (020-8940 3521; www.theteabox.co.uk; Richmond rail/tube; Mon-Thu, Sat-Sun 9am-6.30pm, Fri 9am-10pm).

The Tea Rooms

The Tea Rooms in Stoke Newington are a sanctuary from the hustle and bustle of London life and a delightful venue for morning or afternoon tea. The rooms are an oasis of calm – the bright pastel shades,

antique mirrors and old-fashioned fashion prints, bunting, vintage china and bric-a-brac are guaranteed to transport you to a gentler, bygone age.

All food at the Tea Rooms is handmade, homemade and locally sourced – with an emphasis on quality and taste – by Isabelle and Will, who between them have many years' experience as pastry chefs. The star performer at the Tea Rooms is traditional 'afternoon' tea (served all day, with a glass of prosecco) which includes tasty finger sandwiches, delicious scones with clotted cream and homemade jam, a wide variety of scrumptious cakes and pastries (some are gluten-free), and a fine selection of loose-leaf teas. There's also an array of homemade lunches and hot meals, complete with smaller portions for children.

The Tea Rooms also have a book club, where you can discuss your latest read over a cuppa.

The Tea Rooms, 155 Stoke Newington Church St, N16 0UH (020-7923 1870, www.thetearooms. org, Stoke Newington rail, Tue-Fri 11am-6pm, Sat-Sun 11am-6.30pm, closed Mon).

Tea & Tattle

Located opposite the British Museum, Tea & Tattle is a unique combination of tearoom, gallery and the bookshop Arthur Probsthain (established in 1903), specialising in books about Africa, Asia and the Middle East. Downstairs is the tranquil tearoom, decorated in traditional style with oriental wallpaper, and arranged with charmingly mismatched furniture.

T&T offers an excellent range of leaf teas, including Taiwanese oolong, Japanese sencha, Kenyan fannings, broken orange pekoe from Sri Lanka and Assam (India), accompanied by a selection of cakes, scones and sandwiches – or treat yourself to full afternoon tea. Peaceful and reasonably priced, it's the perfect sanctuary.

Tea & Tattle, 41 Great Russell St, WC1B 3PE (07722-192703; www.apandtea.co.uk; Holborn/ Tottenham Ct Rd tube; Mon-Fri 9-6.30, Sat noon to 4pm, closed Sun).

The Tea House Theatre

Founded in 2011, the Tea House Theatre in Vauxhall is a cosy café by day, mutating seamlessly into a performance space in the evening when a wide variety of entertainment is staged including debating, storytelling, poetry, jazz, films and plays.

The folk here are *very* serious about tea and offer a huge selection of loose-leaf teas, including black, green, oolong, pu'er, white and herbal infusions – even builder's brew! It's also open for breakfast (including full English, Scottish and Ulster fry), lunch and afternoon tea, with scrumptious cakes and sweets such as sticky toffee pudding and homemade rhubarb crumble on the menu. Plus free newspapers and wifi – brilliant!

Tea House Theatre, 139 Vauxhall Walk, SE11 5HL (020-7207 4585; www.teahousetheatre. co.uk; Vauxhall tube; Mon-Sat 8am-8pm, Sun 10am-8pm).

To a Tea

Tucked beneath an office block in Farringdon, not far from St Paul's Cathedral, is To a Tea. Not your usual quaint traditional tea house, it's more of a tea emporium and a magnet for tea lovers. Their own-brand loose-leaf teas are displayed in a grand floor-to-ceiling wall display of some 30 different teas and blends, including black, green (gunpowder green tea), oolong, white (white silver needles and white peony) and herbal infusions, such as liquorice, rose buds and stinging nettle. There are also iced teas.

There's a wide selection of tempting homemade cakes and pastries on offer, including scones, crumpets and cupcakes, plus sandwiches, salads and soups. Good value, too.

To a Tea, 14 Farringdon St, EC4A 4AB (020-7248 3498; http://toatea.com; Farringdon rail/St Paul's tube; Mon-Thu 7.30am-6pm, Fri 7.30-5pm, closed weekends).

Twinings Tea Shop

Twinings was founded in 1706 when Thomas Twining bought the old Tom's Coffee House and daringly introduced tea, which was then an exotic oriental drink. Today Mr Twining's shop (opposite the Royal Courts of Justice) is the oldest in the City of Westminster and incorporates a museum telling the 300-year-old story of the Twining family.

In addition to selling the complete range of Twinings teas, from the everyday to the exotic, the shop also offers a loose tea bar where you can handle, smell and taste dry tea, and a sampling counter where you can enjoy free tastings. You can even become a 'Twinings tea taster' (see website).

Twinings Tea Shop & Museum, 216 The Strand, WC2R 1AP (020-7353 3511; shop.twinings.co.uk/shop/strand; Temple tube; Mon-Fri, 9.30am-7pm, Sat 10am-5pm, Sun 10.30am-4.30pm).

Urban Tea Rooms

A modern twist on the traditional tearoom, Urban serves gourmet tea, Fairtrade coffee and artisan grub by day, while in the evening the basement becomes a funky wine-cum-cocktail bar. Teas are supplied by the Rare Tea Company – including tea from the Tregothnan estate in Cornwall – and served in individual teapots with bone china cups.

The food is British, organic where possible, and includes superior sandwiches and salads, artisan cakes, pastries and breads, while in the evening the menu showcases British 'tapas'. With ample seating, friendly staff and quality refreshments, Urban Tea Rooms is a gem.

Urban Tea Rooms, 19 Kingly St, W1B 5PY (020-7434 3767; http://urbantearooms.com; Oxford Circus tube; Mon 7.30am-6pm, Tue 7.30am-10pm, Wed-Fri 7.30am-11.30pm, Sat 10am-11.30pm, Sun noon-7pm).

Yumchaa

From small beginnings as a stall in Portobello Market, swiftly followed by another in Camden Lock, Yumchaa – it means 'drink tea' in Cantonese – now has five teashops: Camden Market (featured here), Camden Parkway, King's Cross Granary Square, Soho and Tottenham Street.

Although it's at the heart of a busy market, the intimate, rustic teashop is a haven from the surrounding clamour, with a covered balcony overlooking Regent's Canal and West Yard market. The quaint shop serves a wide variety of leaf teas and delicious cakes, muffins, scones, sandwiches and salads. Yummy indeed!

Yumchaa, 91/92 Camden Lock Pl, Upper Walkway, West Yard, NW1 8AF (020-7209 9641; www.yumchaa.com; Camden Town tube; Mon-Fri 9am-6pm, Sat-Sun 9am-6.30pm).

4. Afternoon Tea

The quintessential English pastime of taking afternoon tea is thought to have originated in the mid-1840s with Anna Russell, 7th Duchess of Bedford. While visiting the 5th Duke of Rutland at Belvoir Castle, the custom of serving only two main meals a day – breakfast and dinner (at around 8pm) – left the Duchess feeling hungry by late afternoon, so she would order tea, bread and butter and cakes to be served in her room. The ritual soon spread throughout high society and even caught Queen Victoria's fancy.

Today afternoon tea – exquisite, delicate teas accompanied by divine cakes, pastries and savouries – is something of a phenomenon. This is particularly so in London, where it is popular with both Londoners and visitors and served at hundreds of venues, including restaurants, tearooms, cafés and luxury hotels, which compete to lay on the most lavish and exotic spread.

This chapter includes over 25 of the capital's best afternoon tea venues, ranging from intimate tearooms to five-star hotels, and from a basic cream tea for around £10 to a sublime champagne afternoon tea costing £50 or more.

> Afternoon tea shouldn't be confused with high tea, which refers to a traditional evening meal of the working classes, typically eaten between 5 and 7pm, and consisting of a hot dish followed by bread, butter and cake.

Bake-a-Boo

Acclaimed as the 'best afternoon tea in North London' in 2014 by Time Out, Bake-a-Boo is a cute 'bake shop, tearoom and party parlour' in West Hampstead. The pretty pink teashop is unashamedly traditional with doilies, net curtains and grandma chic galore, and is a lovely venue for a girly get-together.

The traditional afternoon comprises a choice of around 15 teas plus finger sandwiches, scones, cupcakes, chocolate dipped strawberries, mini brownies and shortbread biscuits – with an optional glass of champagne or prosecco. Bake-a-Boo's USP is its range of 'sensitive' afternoon teas – gluten-free, vegan or sugar-free – which are just as delicious as the real McCoy. It also caters for tea parties for every occasion.

Bake-a-Boo, 86 Mill Ln, NW6 1NL (020-7435 1666; www.bake-a-boo.com; W Hampstead/ Kilburn tube; Fri, Sun noon-6pm, Sat 10am-6pm; from £18.50).

The Balcon Hotel

Indulge in a delicious afternoon tea in the elegant Rose Lounge of the Balcon Hotel (formerly Sofitel St James's), a hidden gem in posh St James's. Decorated in pink and cream with stunning displays of fragrant roses, the setting is enhanced by the gentle sound of a harp, making it the perfect spot for a relaxing afternoon tea.

The hotel's French-inspired *Le Tea en Rose* offers a wide choice of brews, ranging from black to green, light to spicy and smoky (such as China green tea gunpowder), herbal infusions to rare, seasonal teas. They're complemented by a selection of finger sandwiches, freshly-baked homemade scones, delicate French pastries, plus an optional cocktail or glass of champagne. *Parfait* – and excellent value, too!

Rose Lounge, Balcon Hotel, 6 Waterloo Pl, SW1Y 5NG (020-7389 7820; www. thebalconlondon.com/roselounge/roselounge. shtm; Charing Cross tube; daily 2.30-5.30pm; from £28).

Baskervilles Tea Shop

A lovely, old-fashioned teashop overlooking Broomfield Park in Palmers Green, Baskervilles is passionate about its teas and cakes. There's a wide range of teas, each blended to their specification by a master tea blender, including black, green and white teas to suit every mood and occasion.

Afternoon tea – which, weather permitting, can be enjoyed in the beautiful tranquil garden – features perennial favourites such as Victoria sponge, chocolate sponge, cupcakes, lemon drizzle, orange and almond cake and chocolate brownies, plus a selection of dairy-, gluten- and wheat-free cakes. You can also buy teas to enjoy at home.

Baskervilles Tea Shop, 66 Aldermans Hill, N13 4PP (020-8351 1673; www.baskervillesteashop. co.uk; Palmers Grn rail/Arnos Grove tube; Mon-Sat 9am-5.30pm, Sun 10am-5pm; £19.50).

BB Bakery

S ituated in the heart of Covent Garden, BB Bakery is the brainchild of Philippe and Brigitte Bloch from France, who opened their authentic French boutique bakery (check out the fabulous cake counter) and *salon de thé* in 2012.

The scrumptious afternoon tea (with optional champagne) is served in the delightful pastel-painted tearoom, and includes a selection of sandwiches and cakes including macaroons, meringues, petits choux, mini cupcakes and scones with clotted cream, as well as a huge choice of loose-leaf teas from Bertjeman & Barton. Gluten-free, vegetarian and halal afternoon teas are also available. The team also offer afternoon tea bus and boat tours and take-away picnic boxes.

BB Bakery, 6-7 Chandos Pl, WC2N 4HU (020-3026 1188; www.bbbakery. co.uk/afternoon-tea; Leicester Sq tube; Mon 10am-7pm, Tue-Sat 9am-8pm, Sun 10am-7pm; from £29).

The Berkeley

The appropriately themed Caramel Room – low-lighting, chocolate-hued walls and faux-crocodile fabrics – is the setting for one of London's more unusual afternoon teas. The Berkeley's award-winning fashionista's afternoon tea, Prêt-à-Portea, is inspired by the themes and colours of the fashion world, with a menu that changes every six months with the fashion seasons.

Tea consists of a selection of loose-leaf teas and a range of delicious cakes, pastries and savouries modelled on the season's colours and the styles of the world's leading designers. Past creations have included honeycomb cream dresses topped with a marzipan bee (based on a design by Alexander McQueen), pistachio panna cotta dresses (Dolce & Gabbana) and Manolo Blahnik slingback chocolate biscuit heels.

The Autumn/ Winter 2015- 2016 Prêt-à-Portea collection took inspiration from an array of distinguished fashion designers, including Dolce & Gabbana's popular pink rose dress from their ground breaking 'Viva La Mama' collection (as seen on the covers of Vogue and Harper's Bazaar). Further delectable details included a take on Moschino's quirky cartoon inspired nu-rave dress and Valentino's rockstud striped shoulder bag. A mouth-watering selection of miniature savoury skewers, taster spoons, elegant canapés and tea sandwiches – a scrumptious tour de force!

The Berkeley, Wilton Pl, SW1X 7RL (020-7107 8866; www.the-berkeley.co.uk/fashion-afternoon-tea; Hyde Park Cnr tube; Mon-Thu 1.45-5.30pm, Fri-Sun 1-5.30pm; from £45).

Blakes Hotel

Blakes – one of the world's first luxury boutique hotels – opened in 1978 in a group of Victorian houses in Kensington. Created by internationally renowned designer Anouska Hempel, it's noted for its super-chic design, service and privacy. Blakes' decor encompasses an atlas of influences, reflected in the abundance and luxury of accessories, furniture and artefacts sourced from around the world.

Afternoon tea at Blakes is served in the subterranean and sensuous splendour of the stunning 'opium den' that is the Chinese Room, adorned with luxurious soft furnishings and Chinese objects, the epitome of decadence and comfort, or – even better – in the beautiful and soothing tranquil oasis of the Japanese Garden.

The splendid afternoon tea is a playful mix of Asian and Anglo touches, including creative sandwiches served bento box-style in a clear Perspex cube, homemade scones with fresh strawberries and clotted cream, and a selection of indulgent cakes. You can choose from a range of loose-leaf teas such as Darjeeling, freshly-brewed ginger or white silver needle or indulge yourself with an optional glass of champagne. Excellent value considering the lavish surroundings.

Blakes Hotel, 33 Roland Gdns, SW7 3PF (020-7370 6701; www.blakeshotels.com; Gloucester Rd tube; daily 3-5pm; from £19).

Bond & Brook

Secreted in the ladies' fashion department on the second floor of Fenwick on Bond Street, Bond & Brook is an elegant restaurant/bar serving breakfast, lunch and afternoon tea. The all-white room is adorned with a burnished pewter bar and is a lovely peaceful retreat – far removed from the hubbub of the store – in which to enjoy afternoon tea (champagne optional).

There's a wide choice of teas served in a silver teapot accompanied by freshly-baked scones, delicious 'couture' cakes and a good selection of finger sandwiches. Push the boat out for the 'luxury' option (book a day in advance) if you want a super-indulgent treat.

Bond & Brook, Fenwick, 2nd floor, 63 New Bond St, W1S 1RQ (020-7629 0273; www. fenwick.co.uk/stores/bond-street/bond-and-brook; Bond St tube; daily from 3pm, except Sun; from £19.50).

Brown's Hotel

One of London's most elegant hotels, historic Brown's is where Queen Victoria used to take tea. The English Tea Room remains one of London's most fashionable tea venues, combining period features – wood panelling, open fires and intricate Jacobean ceilings – with comfortable sofas and armchairs and a background of soft piano music.

The traditional afternoon tea (with optional champagne) is superb, and for the health-conscious there's a tea-tox 'healthy' option that's a lighter (low-carb, low-fat, low-sugar) take on this timeless treat. Brown's has its own 'tea library' and diners are entitled to as many refills (tea, cakes, sandwiches and scones) as desired. Impeccable service and superb quality, too.

Brown's Hotel, Albemarle St, W1S 4BP (020-7518 4155; www.roccofortehotels.com/hotels-and-resorts/browns-hotel/restaurants-and-bars/english-tea-room; Green Pk tube; daily noon-6pm; from £45).

Claridge's

Serving afternoon tea to discerning clients for the best part of 150 years, Claridge's hotel claims to offer 'the English tea of your wildest imagination'. Set in the splendour of the magnificent foyer – inspired by the '20s heyday of Art Deco – the rarefied and refined atmosphere is enhanced by the soothing sounds of a pianist/cellist duo.

There are some 25 specially-blended teas on offer (try the second flush muscatel Darjeeling or the mystical royal white-silver needles, picked at dawn on just two days of the year) accompanied by scrummy scones (with clotted cream and tea-infused jam), perfect pastries and cakes, and delectable sandwiches. This is somewhere to celebrate a special occasion with a special person.

Claridge's, 49 Brook St, Mayfair, W1K 4HR (020-7629 8860; www.claridges.co.uk/mayfair-restaurants-bars/london-afternoon-tea; Bond St tube; daily 2.45-5.30pm; from £55).

Cocomaya

Most famous for its chocolate confections, Cocomaya opened a bakery in 2009 which has garnered a huge and loyal following due to its beautiful and delicious delicacies (not to mention its breakfast/brunch, lunch and afternoon tea menus). Afternoon tea – taken in the bijou rustic shop or at a pavement table on sunny days – is a diet-destroying delight.

For afternoon tea you can choose from a selection of teas and a wealth of sandwiches, cakes, pastries and teasers from next door's chocolate shop, along with cheese straws, freshly-baked scones, mini flour-less chocolate cakes, fudge brownies, blackberry mini loafs, and lemon and poppy-seed cakes. Absolutely divine and excellent value.

Cocomaya, 12 Connaught St, W2 2AF (020-7706 4214/3279; www.cocomaya.co.uk; Marble Arch tube; daily 8am-4pm; around £25).

The Connaught

Awarded the coveted Afternoon Tea Award of Excellence from the Tea Guild in 2013, the Connaught hotel in Mayfair is one of London's grandest tea venues, blending timeless elegance and city chic. Tea is served in the Espelette restaurant, a lovely setting (with a resident harpist) enjoying sweeping views of Mount Street and Tadao Ando's water feature, 'Silence'.

Traditional afternoon tea (with optional champagne) consists of a wide choice of classic and flavoured teas (from imperial Earl Grey or French vanilla to Japanese sencha green), finger sandwiches, scones with clotted cream and a selection of hand-crafted jams. It's finished off with an array of yummy cakes and pastries from patissier Kirk Whittle.

The Connaught, Carlos Pl, W1K 2AL (020-7107 8861; www.the-connaught.co.uk/mayfair-restaurants/london-afternoon-tea; Bond St tube; Mon-Fri 3-5.30pm, Sat-Sun 1-5.30pm; from £45).

The Dorchester

A multiple winner of the Tea Guild's special Award of Excellence, afternoon tea at the Dorchester hotel is a special occasion, served in the luxurious Promenade lobby awash with potted palms and flowering plants, marble columns and plush couches with divinely soft pillows.

In addition to traditional afternoon tea there's 'high tea' (with a light main course and champagne) and champagne afternoon tea, plus a variety of special seasonal afternoon teas including (summer) ice cream afternoon tea, Wimbledon afternoon tea and the Mad Hatter's afternoon tea. You can also have champagne afternoon tea (or spa cocktails) in the Spatisserie in the intimate Dorchester Spa. Go on, spoil yourself...

The Dorchester, Park Ln, W1K 1QA (020-7629 8888; www.dorchestercollection.com/ en/london/the-dorchester/restaurants-bars/ afternoon-tea; Hyde Pk Cnr tube; daily 1-5.30pm; from £49).

Fortnum & Mason

A world-famous food emporium in Piccadilly, Fortnum & Mason (est. 1707) is a combination of delicatessen, department store, restaurant and living museum. Tea is served in the elegant green and blue Diamond Jubilee Tea Salon (opened by HM the Queen in 2012), where a pianist plays soothing tunes.

Fortnum's takes its tea **very** seriously – they offer some 80 different teas – and have expert 'tearistas' (a tea barista) on hand to advise and offer a complimentary tea-tasting session before you order. The beautiful table settings, with silver tea strainers and their trademark duck egg blue porcelain, are more than matched by the delectable food, which includes finger sandwiches, cakes (the chocolate and cherry is heavenly), pastries and scones. A national treasure.

Fortnum & Mason, 181 Piccadilly, W1A 1ER (020-7734 8040; www.fortnumandmason.com/restaurants/afternoon-tea; Green Pk/Piccadilly tube; Mon-Sat noon-7pm, Sun noon-6pm; from £46).

The Goring

The five-star Goring hotel has been serving afternoon tea since opening its doors over 100 years ago. It has long been a favourite with royalty, including the late Queen Mother, and is a holder of the Tea Guild's top London Afternoon Tea Award and Award of Excellence.

Afternoon tea is served in the luxurious bar and lounge, although guests can take their tea on the terrace overlooking the gardens or outside on the veranda in summer. Traditional afternoon tea consists of delicious pastries (gluten-free options available), homemade scones and jams, delicate finger sandwiches and a wide range of first-flush teas from around the world, with an optional glass of Bollinger champagne. Magnificent!

The Goring, 15 Beeston Pl, SW1W 0JW (020-7396 9000; www.thegoring.com/food-drink/afternoon-tea; Victoria tube; daily 3-4pm, Sat 1-4pm; from £42.50).

Grand Imperial

For afternoon tea with a difference – i.e. nothing like traditional afternoon tea – the Grand Imperial's Oriental Afternoon Tea is hard to beat. Served in the plush bar lounge (decorated in burnished gold on black and white), the Oriental tea comes with a variety of mouth-watering dim sum courses (best eaten with chopsticks) arrayed on a beautiful cake stand.

Offerings include a selection of Hong Kong Cantonese delicacies – wasabi prawn dumpling, crispy aromatic duck roll, pumpkin and seafood dumpling, crispy soft shell crab, mixed vegetable lettuce wrap, black cod rolls wrapped in kataifi pastry, steamed barbecue pork buns – followed by sweet treats such as crispy water chestnut roll, oven-baked egg tart and chocolate dim sum creations. Not surprisingly, the highlight is the extensive selection of exotic Chinese teas which include classic jasmine king tea, fermented tea from Yunnan, oolong cha wang (with a delectable white-blossom scent) and tea made from osmanthus flowers.

Oriental tea is served daily from noon until 4.30pm – so you can have it for lunch – and is very reasonably priced. Tea fit for an Empress!

Grand Imperial, The Grosvenor Hotel, 101 Buckingham Palace Rd, SW1W 0SJ (020-7821 8898; www.grandimperiallondon.com/menus/oriental-afternoon-tea; Victoria tube/rail; daily noon-4.30pm; from £28 for two).

Harvey Nichols

The Fifth Floor Café at the top of Harvey Nichols' flagship store in Knightsbridge provides the perfect relaxed setting for a spot of afternoon tea, particularly when the weather's fine and you can enjoy tea on the outdoor terrace.

In addition to a wide choice of traditional and exotic teas to suit all tastes there's a selection of homemade sandwiches, freshly-baked scones with clotted cream and preserves, a range of irresistible cakes and pastries, and indulgent desserts, plus optional house champagne. And with Harvey Nicks' reputation for elegance and style, you can be assured that tea will look every bit as good as it tastes.

Harvey Nichols, Fifth Floor Café, 109-125 Knightsbridge, SW1X 7RJ (020-7235 5250; www.harveynichols.com/news/2015/07/13/ afternoon-tea-london; Knightsbridge tube; daily 3-6pm; from £30).

The Langham

Famous as the birthplace of afternoon tea in London, the glorious Palm Court at the Langham has been serving tea to the cream of London society for over 150 years. The Palm Court is a beautiful room that evokes all the elegance and gentility (with obligatory tinkling piano) that you'd expect from the five-star Langham hotel.

Created by Cherish Finden – multi award-winning executive pastry chef – the Wedgwood Afternoon Tea is a bespoke version of the traditional tea, inspired by Wedgwood porcelain and served in tailor-made 'Langham Rose' Wedgwood teaware. It includes a selection of some 40 tea blends, beautiful cakes and pastries, scrumptious scones and delicate finger sandwiches.

The Langham, 1C Portland Pl, Regent St, W1B 1JA (020-7636 1000; www.langhamhotels.com/ en/the-langham/london/dining/palm-court; Oxford Circus; daily noon-5.30pm; from £49).

Mo Café

Mo Café is the café division of the acclaimed Momo restaurant, a modern Moroccan souk offering superb North African cooking and one of London's most exotic interiors. The café specialises in Moroccan afternoon tea – one of the city's most unusual and tasty treats – served on the inviting terrace or in the chic café-souk next to the main restaurant.

Tea consists of a substantial selection of savoury and sweet bites served on a tall tiered stand – and not a cucumber sandwich in sight. Savouries include Moroccan chicken wrap

filled with a classic Moroccan *chermoula* (garlic and herb paste), cheese *briouats* (deep-fried puff pastries), and *zaalouk* and *mechouia* (smoked aubergine and roast peppers) served on toast. The mouth-watering sweets include *Maghrebine* pastries (date, almond and sesame), a chocolate brownie with chocolate mousse and a pistachio macaroon, followed by a basket of scones with strawberry and fig jam and clotted cream.

The tea menu has a rainbow of choices, and includes exotic flavours such as Empereur Chen-Nung (a smoky China black tea), jasmin mandarine (a flowery green), Blanc & Rose (a white tea with oriental rose petals) and rouge bourbon (vanilla red tea). Classic mint tea is available, too, and all is served in lovely English teacups.

Mo Café, 25 Heddon St, W1B 4BH (020-7434 4040; http://momoresto.com; Oxford/Piccadilly Circus tube; daily 12.30-5.30pm; from £22).

The Orangery, Kensington Gardens

The Orangery in Kensington Gardens is one of the most idyllic settings for afternoon tea in London, with a lovely terrace offering panoramic views of Kensington Palace and its gardens. The Orangery was once the

setting for Queen Anne's glittering court entertainment and its soaring vaulted ceilings, imposing Corinthian columns and classical 18th-century architecture are a magnificent backdrop for afternoon tea.

The English orangery afternoon tea consists of an assortment of sandwiches, wraps and rolls, including smoked salmon and cream cheese, egg mayonnaise and cress, Coronation chicken and, of course, cucumber and mint. They're accompanied by orange-scented and currant studded scones served with Cornish clotted cream and English strawberry jam, and an assortment of cakes and pastries. There's also a gluten-free option and a 'royal' tea with a glass of champagne or sparkling wine.

The range of loose-leaf black and green teas include Royal London Blend (combining the finest single estate Yunnan and Ceylon black teas), Palace Breakfast (an energising, full-bodied blend of Assam and Ceylon) and Afternoon at the Palace (a lighter blend of Darjeeling and China teas). There are herbal and fruit infusions, too.

The magical setting is hard to beat – and it's also excellent value.

Kensington Palace, Kensington Gdns, W8 4PX (020-3166 6112; www.hrp.org.uk/ kensingtonpalace/foodanddrink/orangery; High St Kensington/Queensway tube; daily noon-5pm; from £28).

The Original Maids of Honour

Just a stone's throw from the gates of Kew Gardens, the Original Maids of Honour is a charming traditional teashop steeped in history. The lovely '40s mock Tudor building (the original Victorian building was destroyed in WWII) houses a delightful old-fashioned tearoom with china knick-knacks, blue and white patterned plates, three-tier cake stands and doilies.

Quintessentially English, it's named after the melt-in-the-mouth cake (right) that allegedly took Henry VIII's fancy when he found Ann Boleyn and the other Maids of Honour scoffing them at Richmond Palace. The recipe is a well-kept secret to this day, but they appear to have a puff pastry base, a layer of curd and a topping of (cheddar?) cheese – delicious and very moreish.

The Original Maids of Honour is first and foremost a traditional bakery, dating back to 1887, with everything made and baked on the premises using fresh, natural ingredients – including a mouth-watering selection of cakes and pastries. The teashop offers a range of set teas (best after 2pm) ranging from a simple cream tea through Maids of Honour afternoon tea, English afternoon tea and high tea, to the pièce de résistance: champagne high tea.

The Original Maids of Honour, 288 Kew Rd, TW9 3DU (020-8940 2752; www. theoriginalmaidsofhonour.co.uk; Kew Gardens tube; daily 8.30am-6pm; from £20 for two).

The Oxo Tower Brasserie

Southwark landmark the OXO Tower was originally constructed as a power station, and was acquired by the manufacturers of OXO beef stock cubes who rebuilt it to an Art Deco design in the '20s. After falling into disrepair it was refurbished in the '90s as a mixed use development, with the OXO Tower

Restaurant, Bar and Brasserie (operated by Harvey Nichols) on the rooftop. The tower is a splendid sight and prominent landmark – particularly at night when the OXO letters are lit up in red – offering unparalleled views across the City's skyline.

You can enjoy afternoon tea with a difference at the OXO Tower Brasserie. The difference is that it's called 'Not Afternoon Tea' and consists of four tasting dessert plates with a matching bespoke cocktail –

and not a teacup in sight! You can choose from four themes which are regularly updated, e.g. Rhubarb, Rhubarb, Rhubarb, exploring the marvellous versatility of this tasty plant, Nuts About Chocolate aimed at diehard chocoholics, Fun Fair with popcorn and candyfloss favours, or Tea Party, a selection of tea-tinged sweet concoctions. And if that's not eccentric enough, opt for Alice's Adventures in Wonderland, a curiouser and curiouser take on afternoon tea.

The OXO Tower Brasserie, OXO Tower Wharf, Barge House St, SE1 9PH (020-7803 3888, www. harveynichols.com/restaurants/oxo-tower-london, Waterloo tube, Mon-Fri 3-4.30pm; from £26).

The Ritz

Served since 1906, afternoon tea at the Ritz hotel is regarded by many as the quintessential English tea 'ceremony'. It's impeccably served in the spectacular Palm Court – originally called the Winter Garden – a dramatic, elegant salon of fanciful design, flanked by walls of mirrors, a ceiling of intricate gilded trellis design, marble pillars, birdcage chandeliers with ornate metal flowers, a striking stone fountain with gilded statues, fronded palms and a stunning central floral display.

Tea at the Ritz is formal and theatrical: you take your place on the Palm Court's 'stage', which is populated by elegantly-dressed guests and immaculate waiters flitting among the tables set with delicate fine bone china and gleaming silver tea services, against a backdrop of soothing music from the resident pianist or string quartet.

The menu is classic and traditional: a selection of around 16 loose-leaf teas; delicate finger sandwiches with traditional fillings such as smoked salmon, cucumber, egg, roast ham and cheese; a daily selection of scrumptious tea cakes and pastries; and freshly-baked raisin and apple scones with strawberry preserve and Devonshire clotted cream. For a special occasion you can order the celebration tea, which includes an appropriate cake. Pure indulgence and unforgettable – but book well in advance.

The Ritz, 150 Piccadilly, W1J 9BR (020-7300 2345; www.theritzlondon.com/palm-court; Green Pk tube; daily 11.30am-9pm; from £50).

The Shard

Afternoon tea at the Shard – the tallest building in Europe – gives a whole new meaning to the term 'high tea'. Three restaurants offer a tea service, all offering breath-taking views of the London skyline.

The **Aqua Shard** (020-3011 1256; Mon-Fri 3-5pm; from £42) offers a contemporary English afternoon tea with a modern twist, served in the restaurant's atrium located on the 31st floor. Tea includes delicious finger sandwiches such as Earl Grey tea-smoked Loch Duart salmon with caviar and dill-scented cream, while sweet delights include lemon meringue tart and cassis and yoghurt panna cotta.

Gông at Shangri-La Hotel (020-7234 8208; daily 2-4pm; from £49) on the 52nd floor of the Shard takes afternoon tea to new heights, with interiors reminiscent of a traditional boudoir. The classic afternoon tea menu includes freshly-cut sandwiches, homemade pastries, Earl Grey and scones with Cornish clotted cream and strawberry jam, plus stunning sweet confections such as yuzu cheese cake.

The contemporary, Chinese-style **Ting Lounge at Shangri-La** (020-7234 8108; Mon-Fri 2-6.30pm, Sat-Sun noon-4pm, from £49) on the 35th floor has both a classic English and an Asian-inspired afternoon tea, the latter comprising oriental-flavoured sweet treats and savouries, including freshly-steamed dumplings and roast duck.

Each tea is far from cheap, but worth it for the amazing panoramic views – and it saves you paying a hefty price (£25.95!) to visit the viewing platform.

The Shard, 32 London Bridge St, SE1 9SG (www.the-shard.com/restaurants; London Br tube).

Sketch

If you want afternoon tea with a wow factor, Sketch is hard to beat. A fashionable venue for food, art and music, the traditional afternoon tea menu – created by Michelin-starred chef Pierre Gagnaire – is served in two very different rooms: the Glade, a fairy-tale dining room featuring ethereal woodland murals and wicker furnishings, and the Gallery, a breath-taking room in stunning pink velvet designed by India Mahdavi, with provocative art by David Shrigley.

The innovative afternoon tea – with optional (if irresistible) champagne – offers a choice of around 20 teas (by Jing) and a show-stopping assortment of sweet pastries (raspberry meringues, bubble gum marshmallows), dainty macaroons decorated with rose petals, and delicious finger sandwiches (e.g. caviar and quail's egg) and savouries. Don't forget to visit the stunning egg-pod loos!

Sketch, 9 Conduit St, W1S 2XG (020-7659 4500; http://sketch.london; Oxford Circus tube; daily 12.30-4.30pm; from £39).

Teanamu Chaya Teahouse

The Teanamu Chaya Teahouse offers a unique afternoon tea with an Asian twist in a serene and calm hideaway off bustling Portobello Road. Entering tea master Pei Wang's quaint teahouse is to be instantly soothed. Here 'taking tea' is an intimate and ceremonial experience – and much healthier than the sugar-laden traditional English treat.

Savour delicate, handmade patisserie and delectable Chinese dim sum, such  as kumquat ginger preserve and mature cheddar sandwiches, vegetarian dumplings with chilli oil, mango seed cake and peanut sesame cookies, and olive oil lemon cake with mango curd, accompanied by a choice of elegant Chinese and Japanese teas.

Teanamu Chaya Teahouse, Coach House, 14A St Luke's Rd, W11 1DP (020-7243 0374; www. teanamu.com/teahouse; Westbourne Pk tube; Sat-Sun noon-6pm; from £25).

The Wolseley

The Wolseley is an elegant café-restaurant in the grand European tradition, occupying the former car showroom of Wolseley Motors designed in the '20s by William Curtis Green. The architect drew on Venetian and Florentine influences with exotic Eastern touches to create a majestic interior with marble floors, towering Corinthian pillars, grand arches and sweeping stairways – it's one of London's most beautiful and atmospheric spaces.

Afternoon tea is served in the cosy café, where there's a more casual atmosphere than in the main dining room, although its service is just as polished. It effortlessly blends English tradition with the quintessential European feel of the restaurant, and manages to offer a more modern (and cheaper) alternative to its glamourous neighbour, the Ritz.

Tea consists of lavish stacks of finger sandwiches, fruit scones and a selection of scrumptious cakes (such as Battenberg or Sachertorte), accompanied by a pot of tea of your choice (although not as extensive as some other establishments) and optional champagne. Nice touches are the hourglass timer (to time your tea), silver tea strainers and luxurious linen napkins. Those wanting a lighter option can choose the cream tea. Go for the ambience and the fascinating people-watching.

If hunger strikes early, the Wolseley is also famous for its breakfasts (Mon-Fri 7-11.30am, Sat-Sun 8-11.30am).

The Wolseley, 160 Piccadilly, W1J 9EB (020-7499 6996; www.thewolseley.com/afternoon-tea; Green Pk tube; Mon-Fri 3-6.30pm, Sat 3.30-5.30pm, Sun 3.30-6.30pm; from £25.50).

5. Breakfast/Brunch

The hearty breakfast ranks alongside afternoon tea and the Sunday roast as one of Britain's most famous culinary traditions. The traditional 'full English' – a grand fry-up of eggs, bacon, sausages, etc. – is the perennial favourite, although it's rarely eaten every day. Most people start the day with tea or coffee and toast or cereal, with breakfast blow outs saved for special treats. However, an increasing number of restaurants and cafés are tempting diners with their creative breakfast menus featuring a plethora of inviting dishes, from pancakes with blueberries and avocado on sourdough toast to eggs Benedict and *shakshuka* (poached eggs in a sauce of tomatoes, chilli peppers, onions and spices).

Breakfast usually ends around 11am but brunch – a combination of breakfast and lunch – can extend to 3pm or later and is perfect for convivial grazing. Londoners have taken to it with a passion and many venues specialise in serving brunch, particularly at weekends, offering a range of irresistible dishes from breakfast classics to hearty mains and tempting puds – not forgetting the odd cocktail.

This chapter features over 25 of the city's best breakfast and/or brunch venues, ranging from luxury hotels to cosy cafés, posh restaurants to traditional diners, and Parisienne-style brasseries to artisan bakeries.

Brunch originated in England in the late 1800s, when it was often served buffet style. In 1895, *Punch* magazine described it as 'a Sunday meal for Saturday-night carousers'!

Aubaine

Housed in a spacious corner building in the heart of Marylebone, Aubaine is an all-day licensed café-restaurant and a favourite with local folk. Difficult to pigeonhole, it's part of a small chain of around ten which are a seductive blend of cosmopolitan style and French cuisine – Parisian brasserie meets Provençal bistro with the added allure of an in-house boulangerie and patisserie.

It's a must-try for its *petit déjeuner* menu which includes superb French croissants and pastries, granola with yogurt and fruit, eggs Benedict/Florentine/Royale, full French breakfast (Toulouse sausage, Alsace bacon, free range eggs, mushrooms and Provençale haricot beans), *croque monsieur* (or *madame*), French toast and much more.

Brunch features most of the above plus a choice of creative salads and a range

of other delicious dishes, including buffalo *burrata* (creamy mozzarella) with cherry tomatoes, avocado oil and crostini; beef carpaccio with truffle vinaigrette; *feuilleté de chèvre et champignons* (puff pastry, goat's cheese, onion puree, capers, olives, figs and bitter spring leaves); or beef fillet, crispy shallots, French fries and pepper sauce. There's also excellent coffee and a good selection of fine teas from Mariage Frères.

Not the cheapest place for breakfast/brunch – it's Marylebone after all – but one of the best. *Vive les Aubaine!*

Aubaine, 7 Moxon St, W1U 4EP (020-3393 6330; www.aubaine.co.uk/locations/marylebone; Baker St tube, Mon-Sat 8am-10.30pm, Sun 9am-10pm).

Balthazar

Opened in 2013, Balthazar in Covent Garden is a faithful copy of a New York institution, which was itself based on a French brasserie/bistro – hence the red awnings, leather banquettes, giant antique mirrors and mosaic floors. Balthazar serves everything from *tartines* to *moules frites*, but is renowned for its breakfasts (no need to book) and weekend brunch.

The breakfast menu features eggs any way you want them (boiled with Parmesan soldiers, on  toast with avocado, scrambled with Cornish crab) alongside New York pancakes and an authentic full English, while healthier options include date and cherry granola and porridge. The amazing brunch menu adds delicious hors d'oeuvres and entrees (see website). A special place to start the day.

Balthazar, 4-6 Russell St, WC2B 5HZ (020-3301 1155; http://balthazarlondon.com; Covent Gdn tube; breakfast, Mon-Fri 7.30-11am; brunch weekends 10am-4pm).

Bistrotheque

Occupying a converted factory in Bethnal Green, Bistrotheque belies its uninspiring location with its uber-cool vibe. Elegant and contemporary, its décor is pure industrial chic, with high ceilings showcasing sparkling white pipes and beams above white-tiled walls and a long wood-fronted bar.

It's a popular hangout with East End hipsters who flock there to graze on the weekend brunch and listen to live piano music. As well as classics – avocado on toast, pancakes with bacon and maple syrup, eggs every which way – you can sample more unusual dishes such as crab rarebit with rocket and capers, and pig's cheek with Boston baked beans and Dijon mustard. And if you need a hair of the dog, there are divine cocktails. Superb food, reasonably priced – booking recommended.

Bistrotheque, 23-27 Wadeson St, E2 9DR (020-8983 7900; www.bistrotheque.com; Cambridge Heath rail/Bethnal Gn tube; brunch, weekends 11am-4pm).

The Breakfast Club

The appropriately named Breakfast Club is a pretty little egg-yolk yellow café tucked away in Islington's Camden Passage. It's one of eight branches of this mini chain that first opened in Soho in 2005.

Borrowing its theme from a cult '80s movie, the Breakfast Club lives up to its name by serving one of the capital's best breakfasts: try the awesome US-style crispy bacon, perfect eggs and scrummy pancakes. Meanwhile, *Huevos al Benny* – poached eggs, chorizo, roast peppers, avocado, fresh chillies and spicy hollandaise on a toasted muffin – is a guaranteed hangover cure! Best of all, breakfast is served until 5pm every day. Come on Saturday and browse the antiques market, but expect to queue. It's well worth it!

The Breakfast Club, 31 Camden Passage, N1 8EA (020-7226 5454; www. thebreakfastclubcafes.com; Angel tube; Mon-Wed 8am-10pm, Thu-Sat 8am-11pm, Sun 8am-10pm).

Bunnychow

Winner of the UK's Most Innovative Breakfast 2015 (www. shakeupyourwakeup.com/breakfastawards), Bunnychow on Soho's Wardour Street is an innovative eatery serving Durban-style street food known as a Bunny: a hollowed-out bread loaf with assorted fillings.

The eatery's winning entry – the Full English Bunny – consists of a brioche loaf stuffed with sausage, lean bacon, tomato, button mushrooms, salsa beans, black pudding and a fried egg – all for the princely sum of £4.50. What's more you can (allegedly) eat this South African treat without a knife and fork. If this isn't your bag there are lots more tasty fillings, including slow-cooked mutton curry, spicy chicken and tomato, and pulled pork. Soooo tasty – and a bargain to boot.

Bunnychow, 74 Wardour St, W1F 0TE (020-7439 9557; http://bunnychow.com; Piccadilly Circus tube; Mon-Thu 9am-10pm, Fri-Sat 9am-11pm, Sun 10am-7pm).

Caravan

You can eat your way around the world at Caravan, a cool, trendy café-restaurant, bar and coffee roastery in Farringdon's bustling Exmouth Market. With huge windows overlooking the market, the restaurant has an outdoorsy feel which is enhanced during fine weather when the doors roll back. The room has a casual laid-back vibe and funky industrial design – wooden tables, white pipework and trendy light fittings – although the mouth-watering food is the star attraction.

There are three menus – breakfast, brunch and an all-day menu – all offering small and large sharing plates using seasonal ingredients to create inventive dishes featuring flavours from around the globe. The fashionable term is fusion food but don't let that put you off. There are no chicken Balti pizzas here!

Breakfast treats include banana caramel porridge and cream; avocado, olive oil and chilli flakes on sourdough  toast; and smoky black pudding with maple roast apples, fried egg and toast. For brunch, there are orange-scented pancakes with blueberries and vanilla butter; Welsh rarebit on sourdough with a poached egg and onion jam; and cornbread French toast with bacon, rocket and avocado. Coffee is excellent (roasted in house) and wines are interesting and fairly priced.

Innovative Caravan makes fusion food trendy – and anywhere that has 'two crumpets with too much butter' on the menu has to be a winner.

Caravan, 11-13 Exmouth Mkt, EC1R 4QD (020-7833 8115; www.caravanonexmouth.co.uk; Farringdon tube; breakfast, Mon-Fri 8-11.30am; brunch, weekends 10am-4pm).

Colbert

With its prime position on Sloane Square next to the Royal Court Theatre, Colbert is the perfect spot to enjoy breakfast/brunch. This vast all-day grand café – part of the Corbin & King empire – offers a tempting all-day menu which can be enjoyed alfresco at a pavement table (perfect for people-watching) or in the chic dining room.

A light breakfast menu, including organic porridge, granola, avocado on toast and French toast with berries, is served from 8am to noon, while *oeufs* are on the menu all day: choose from fried, scrambled, eggs Benedict/Royale or full English. For a lighter bite, sample something from Colbert's selection of scrumptious Viennoiserie. *Magnifique!*

Colbert, 50-52 Sloane Sq, SW1W 8AX (020-7730 2804; www.colbertchelsea.com; Sloane Sq tube; breakfast/brunch, Mon-Thu 8am-11pm, Fri-Sat 8am-11.30pm, Sun 8am-10.30pm).

Cookbook Café

Those with huge appetites and fat wallets can enjoy the breakfast or brunch of kings at the Cookbook Café in the InterContinental Park Lane. Prices are big (continental £19.50, full English £28) but so is the choice of cereals, yoghurts, compotes, Danish pastries, muffins and juices and, if you go full English, eggs, pancakes, waffles, bacon, sausages and more.

For an even bigger blow-out, try the all-you-can-eat weekend brunch, which, as well as the breakfast goodies, features tapas-style mains, a cold market table (cold cuts, seafood, salads etc.), traditional mains (a Sunday roast) and irresistible desserts. Unlimited drinks include Bellinis and Prosecco. It costs a wallet-busting £52 on Saturdays, £59 on Sundays (under-17s £40, under-12s £25, under-6s free). Starve yourself for a week beforehand…

Cookbook Café, InterContinental Park Lane, 1 Hamilton Pl, Park Ln, W1J 7QY (020-7318 8563; www.cookbookcafe.co.uk; Hyde Pk Cnr tube; breakfast, Mon-Fri 6.30-10.30am, weekends 6.30-11am; brunch, weekends 12.30-3.30pm).

Dean Street Townhouse

A luxury five-star boutique hotel and all-day dining room in the heart of Soho, Dean Street Townhouse occupies a pair of handsome four-storey Georgian townhouses (1732-1735, Grade II listed), once home to the legendary Gargoyle Club. During the 18th century this was something of a cosmopolitan centre, home to sculptors, architects and leading artists including William Hogarth.

The celebrated dining room – classical English design with dark-wood panelling, hardwood floors, striking chandeliers, vintage armchairs and lovely red-leather banquettes, decorated with modern art by leading contemporary British artists – serves breakfast and brunch to all-comers (plus lunch, afternoon tea, and dinner).

Breakfast includes a selection of classic dishes including sausage or bacon sandwich, ham hock hash with fried duck egg, grilled kippers with butter, kedgeree, and crumpets with preserves. There are fruit smoothies for the pious, and Scots will be heartened to see Lorne (square, flat) sausage and tattie scones. There's also a bargain full English of eggs, sausages, bacon, tomato, mushrooms and black pudding.

The excellent weekend brunch includes the all-day breakfast and bakery options plus a choice of starters, salads,  mains, sides and desserts, and a variety of Bloody Marys to help things along. They also do a mean Sunday roast (noon to 6pm). A real star – and good value, too.

Dean Street Townhouse, 69-71 Dean St, W1D 3SE (020-7434 1775; www. deanstreettownhouse.com; Piccadilly Circus tube; breakfast/brunch, Mon-Fri, from 7am, weekends from 8am).

The Delaunay

Indulge yourself with a truly special breakfast or brunch at the elegant Art Deco Delaunay café-restaurant in Covent Garden, which takes its inspiration from the grand cafés of Europe. The glamorous and sophisticated dining room echoes a sumptuous '20s European brasserie with a vibrant cosmopolitan buzz.

The splendid breakfast includes an irresistible array of house-made Viennoiserie; a range of toasted breads with homemade jams and spreads; healthy choices such as Bircher muesli, granola, yoghurt, prunes and fruit salad; and hot breakfast standards including porridge, crispy bacon rolls, sausage sandwiches, pancakes, French toast and eggs (*eier*) however you want them. There's also the obligatory full English or, for something out of the ordinary, try the Viennese breakfast (smoked ham, salami, artisan Gouda, boiled egg and pretzel).

Specials (*Spezialitäten*) include oatmeal soufflé with pear and cranberry compote, and omelette Arnold Bennett. To drink there's a selection of speciality coffees, fine teas, smoothies and juices.

The weekend brunch menu expands to include soups, salads, sandwiches, seafood cocktails, fish, entrées, schnitzels and cheese. Booking recommended. The Delaunay is also the perfect setting for a decadent Viennese-style afternoon tea. A class act.

The Delaunay, 55 Aldwych, WC2B 4BB (020-7499 8558; www.thedelaunay.com; Holborn or Covent Gdn tube; breakfast Mon-Fri 7-11.30am, Sat 8-11am, Sun 9-11am; brunch, weekends 11am-5pm).

Dishoom

A wonderfully kitsch café-restaurant in Shoreditch (one of four London locations), Dishoom is a modern take on the old Irani (Persian) style cafés, popular in '60s Bombay. Its faded retro design incorporates ceiling fans, bamboo blinds, cane furniture, vintage advertising and droll slogans – and it has a lovely Raj-style 'verandah' to relax on.

The Indian-fusion breakfast menu includes delicious naan rolls – spread with cream cheese, chilli tomato jam and fresh herbs, wrapped around fillings of bacon, egg and sausage – *akuri* (spicy scrambled eggs), *kejriwal* (fried eggs on chilli cheese toast) or the Big Bombay (full English). To drink there's breakfast lassi, Bloody Marys, fresh juices, chai (spiced tea) and Malabar coffee – you can even order champagne. Indian heaven!

Dishoom, 7 Boundary St, E2 7JE (020-7420 9324; www.dishoom.com; Shoreditch High St rail; breakfast Mon-Fri 8-11.30am, weekends 9am-noon).

E5 Bakehouse Café

An artisan bakery – best sourdough in London – and coffee shop in East London (E8, strangely), the E5 Bakehouse is built into an archway with tables outside. It serves breakfast and weekend brunch (and lunch) using delicious local, organic produce, with great coffee from Nude Espresso.

Breakfast includes sourdough toast with tasty toppings, healthy house-made granola with Greek yoghurt and fruit, Bircher muesli, croissants and pastries. For weekend brunch there are savoury bakes such as sausage rolls and *spanakopita* (Greek spinach pie), along with dishes such as falafel, robust salads and filling sandwiches, while on Sundays they serve delicious sourdough pizza. Excellent bread-making courses, too.

E5 Bakehouse, Arch 395, Mentmore Ter, E8 3PH (020- 8986 9600; http://e5bakehouse.com; London Fields rail; breakfast, Mon-Fri 6-11am, weekends 6-9am; brunch, weekends 9am-4pm).

The Electric Diner

Enjoy breakfast or brunch in retro surroundings at the Electric Diner, adjacent to the Electric Cinema on Portobello Road. It's a traditional US diner (looking a bit like a railroad car), complete with low lighting, French grey plank ceiling, exposed brick walls, tiled floor and an open kitchen down one side. You can sit on a bar stool or at one of the red-leather booths and listen to an authentic American soundtrack. There's also outside seating for people-watchers.

Breakfast is served from 8am and includes pastries, fruit and yoghurt, porridge, waffles, and eggs any style – try eggs Benedict/Florentine/Royale, omelette with Gruyère, or smoked salmon with scrambled eggs. There's also a full English (with a veggie version). On-trend options include avocado on toast with chilli and poached egg, and hot

smoked salmon with quinoa and goat's cheese. There's a variety of coffees and teas, creamy milkshakes and fruity smoothies. And the newspapers are free.

At noon, breakfast morphs into the all-day French-American brunch menu, incorporating such delights as buttermilk biscuits with mushroom gravy, honey-fried chicken with chili and sesame, and steak and frites. There are also some stunning desserts (knickerbocker glory!), well-mixed cocktails, a thoughtful wine list and a choice of some 20 beers. Reasonably priced and authentically executed – a real slice of American pie.

Electric Diner, 191 Portobello Rd, W11 2ED (020-7908 9696; www.electricdiner.com, Ladbroke Grove tube; breakfast, daily 8am-noon).

The Fox & Anchor

Get up with the larks (well, at 7am) and enjoy a hearty breakfast at The Fox & Anchor, an attractive heritage pub near Smithfield Market with an abundance of dark wood, mosaic tiled floors, etched mirrors and a pewter bar.

Those with the appetites of market traders (or porters) can start the day with the substantial City Boy Breakfast: £16.95 gets you two eggs, sweet cured bacon, two pork and leek sausages, minute steak, lamb's kidney, calves liver, black and white pudding, tomato, mushroom, baked beans, fried bread – and a pint of stout! For the rest of us there's the standard full English (the Full Monty), Welsh rarebit, and a selection of egg dishes, baps and porridge. Tally ho!

The Fox & Anchor, 115 Charterhouse St, EC1M 6AA (020-7250 1300; www.foxandanchor.com; Farringdon tube; breakfast, Mon-Fri 7-11am, weekends 7am-noon).

Gail's Kitchen

Situated in the heart of Bloomsbury, Gail's Kitchen – part of an extensive upmarket bakery chain known for its pastries, cakes and dinky sandwiches – is a smart brasserie that serves a delicious weekend brunch. The bright, modern eatery with white walls, orange banquettes, salvaged wood tables and white wire-framed chairs was awarded a Michelin Bib Gourmand in 2015.

The menu offers a range of classic and contemporary dishes including scrambled eggs, smoked salmon and toasted croissant; banana bread with sour cream and dates; pancakes with streaky bacon, maple syrup and butter; and *shakshuka* (eggs and feta cheese baked in tomato and pepper sauce). Drinks include a brilliant Bloody Mary, summer cup and fresh juices, plus a selection of scrummy desserts. Superb!

Gail's Kitchen, 11-13 Bayley St, WC1B 3HD (020-7323 9694; www.gailskitchen.co.uk; Goodge St tube; brunch, weekends 10am-3pm).

The Good Egg

Starting life as a appealing pop-up and street-food market stall, The Good Egg found a permanent North London home in 2015 and serves one of the best brunches in town. The buzzy all-day menu – a small but tempting array of plates – is an eclectic mix of owner Joel Braham's and his staff's

favourite dishes, inspired by their childhood and travels in Israel and North America. Not surprisingly, it's heavily skewed towards the fashionable (and delicious) Israeli and Middle Eastern food popularised by Yotam Ottolenghi (see page 45).

Brunch stars include challah French toast and date syrup with caramelised banana, sweet *dukkah* (an Egyptian nut-and-spice mix) and optional bacon; Iraqi aubergine pitta stuffed with egg, fried aubergine, *zhoug* (spicy relish), mango amba (pickle) and tahini; breakfast burrito (eggs, chorizo, sauté potatoes, cheese, refried beans, guacamole and hot sauce); and the obligatory moreish *shakshuka* (baked eggs with tomato and peppers).

To drink there's excellent coffee, fresh juices and smoothies, and some great brunch cocktails, including a red hot 'Bloody Mary' with gin and pastrami spices (!), and pickleback: bourbon with a dill pickle brine chaser. Eggcellent food and great value, too. Get cracking!

The Good Egg Co, 93 Stoke Newington Church St, N16 0AS (020-7682 2120; www. thegoodeggco.com; Stoke Newington rail; breakfast Tue-Fri from 9am, brunch weekends from 10am, closed Mon).

Grain Store

Situated on Granary Square in King's Cross – with a huge terrace overlooking Regent's Canal – the award-winning Grain Store occupies a beautiful space with a theatrical 'exploded' kitchen: some of the cooking takes place at the table. The brainchild of chef Bruno Loubet, the eclectic menu gives veggies a starring role, although it isn't a vegetarian restaurant.

Loubet offers an innovative and mouth-watering weekend brunch with such intriguing dishes as compressed watermelon, padrón peppers, pecorino and olive 'truffle'; potato pancake, sour cream leeks, poached duck egg and Tobiko wasabi caviar; beetroot and chocolate cake, pink grapefruit and orange gel; and rice pudding panna cotta, chilli pineapple and miso fudge. Scrumptious, unusual – and good value, too.

Grain Store, Granary Sq, 1-3 Stable St, N1C 4AB (020-7324 4466; www.grainstore.com; King's Cross/St Pancras tube/rail; brunch, weekends 10am-2.45pm).

Granger & Co

The first of three UK outlets from Australian celebrity chef, restaurateur and food author Bill Granger, Granger & Co whips up a bonzer breakfast/brunch. With its bright yellow awnings, light-filled interior and smattering of pavement tables, the Notting Hill restaurant has a relaxed continental feel

The inventive menu offers the usual breakfast favourites, but with an Aussie twist. So your eggs (fried, poached or soft boiled) come with less familiar sides such as miso mushrooms, kimchi or rose harissa. 'Classics' include the Fresh Aussie breakfast: tea-smoked salmon, poached eggs, greens, avocado and cherry tomatoes. There are lighter options such as Bircher muesli and the delightfully named Sunrise smoothie, a blend of berries, banana, apple, yoghurt and orange. Comfort food with a healthy twist!

Granger & Co, 175 Westbourne Grove, W11 2SB (020-7229 9111; http://grangerandco.com; Notting Hill Gate tube; breakfast, Mon-Sat 7am-noon, Sun 8am-noon).

Greenberry Café

A lively café-brasserie in the heart of Primrose Hill, Greenberry Café is the brainchild of well-travelled Welsh-born foodie Morfudd Richards, who cut her teeth at Harvey's (Marco Pierre White), the Ivy and Le Caprice – and was co-owner of Lola's and founder of celebrated Lola's Ice Creams. The bright, homely café – with fashionable exposed brick and wood design palette – offers an eclectic all-day dining menu and is the sort of place where you can drop in for a glass of wine, a snack or a more substantial meal.

Breakfast is served from 9am to 3pm daily and includes standards such as homemade granola, porridge and pancakes. You can have eggs any style – including the irresistible trinity of Benedict, Florentine and Royale – and there's kedgeree or *shakshuka* (spicy baked eggs) available, too. There's also delicious sourdough toast, croissants, pastries and a good choice of coffee (Climpson), tea (Rare Tea Co) and fresh fruit juices – or a Bloody Mary if you prefer.

There's no brunch menu as such but from midday you can also dip into the traiteur menu which includes smoked salmon bagel with cream cheese and dill, and wild rice, quinoa, butternut squash, goat's cheese, mint and pomegranate salad. The dessert 'trolley' beckons with Valrhona gluten-free chocolate brownie and salted caramel ice cream. And remember, Morfudd (Lola) is famous for her ice cream!

Greenberry Café, 101 Regent's Park Rd, NW1 8UR (020-7483 3765; http://greenberrycafe. co.uk; Chalk Farm tube; breakfast/brunch, daily 9am-3pm).

Hawksmoor Guildhall

A steakhouse is perhaps an unusual choice for breakfast, but the Guildhall branch of the celebrated Hawksmoor chain (the only outlet serving breakfast) does probably the best power breakfast in town. With its boardroom-style mahogany panelling and parquet floors it appears targeted at testosterone-filled businessmen needing to fuel their mega-buck deals with a mighty meaty breakfast. It also offers lighter fare such as granola, porridge and grapefruit for the hoi polloi.

Those with gargantuan appetites can order the ultimate Hawksmoor breakfast (£35 for two

to share): a monstrous platter including smoked bacon chop, sausages (made with pork, beef and mutton), black pudding, short-rib, bubble and squeak, grilled bone marrow, trotter baked beans, fried eggs, grilled mushrooms, roast tomatoes, HP gravy and unlimited toast (phew!). The full English at £15 a head isn't much smaller. If that doesn't float your boat there's plenty more to choose from, including steak or bacon chop, fried eggs and hash browns; Manx kipper and poached eggs; smoked salmon with scrambled eggs; and lobster Benedict.

If you need to kick start your day with a hair of the dog, there are various 'anti-fogmatics' (breakfast cocktails) including several Bloody Marys, Shaky Pete's ginger brew, Marmalade cocktail or the ultimate Corpse Reviver No. 2 (gin, Triple Sec, Cocchi Americano, lemon juice and a dash of absinthe). Cheers!

Hawksmoor Guildhall, 10 Basinghall St, EC2V 5BQ (020-7397 8120; http://thehawksmoor.com/locations/guildhall; Bank tube; breakfast, Mon-Fri 7-10am).

Modern Pantry

With a relaxed, calm setting and charming ambience, the Modern Pantry in Clerkenwell is just the place to enjoy an imaginative breakfast or brunch. It's noted for its flavoursome fusion food; chef Anna Hansen's (ex-Providores) culinary philosophy is to excite the palate by tweaking everyday dishes with unusual ingredients – and breakfast is no exception.

Typical offerings include spiced red-wine poached tamarillo with Greek yoghurt and manuka honey; Rendang mince on toast, with a deep fried egg and chilli lime dressing; and Persian chicken burger, with coconut and black sesame labneh, gooseberry relish and cassava chips. The drinks are mind-blowing, too – liquorice and chilli hot chocolate, anyone? A culinary conundrum.

The Modern Pantry, 47-48 St John's Sq, EC1V 4JJ (020-7553 9210; www.themodernpantry. co.uk; Farringdon tube; breakfast, Mon-Fri 8-11am; brunch, Sat 9am-4pm, Sun 10am-4pm).

Pimlico Fresh

In an area that's something of a gastronomic desert, Pimlico Fresh is a ray of Aussie sunshine. This welcoming café, with its large bench tables (plus a few outside) for laidback communal eating and a huge chalkboard menu, dishes up scrumptious homemade delights from breakfast and brunch through to afternoon tea.

The menu isn't vast but has the basics covered: eggs cooked every which way, granola, porridge and French toast, plus special plates such as avocado, chargrilled bacon, cherry tomatoes and wholegrain toast, or baked eggs with chorizo, spinach, feta and tomato. There's also excellent (Monmouth) coffee and tea, fresh juices, smoothies, and a selection of scrummy cakes and pastries. Friendly, efficient service, fantastic food, great value – bonzer!

Pimlico Fresh, 86-87 Wilton Rd, SW1V 1DN (020-7932 0030; Victoria tube/rail; breakfast/ brunch, Mon-Fri from 7.30am, weekends from 9am).

Plum & Spilt Milk

A hidden sanctuary in King's Cross, Plum & Spilt Milk (named after the colours of the Flying Scotsman's dining cars) is secreted away on the first floor of the Great Northern Hotel, which first opened in 1854. Originally designed by master builder Lewis Cubitt, it has been magnificently refurbished. Exquisitely re-designed to evoke the glamour and grace of the iconic building's past, the elegant yet relaxing restaurant features floor-to-ceiling windows, hand-blown hanging pendant lamps, sublime handmade furniture (cream leather banquettes), French navy walls, dark marble table-tops and cut-glass stands.

The achingly cool PSM serves a simple selection of classic breakfast dishes, beautifully cooked and presented courtesy of chef Mark Sargeant. The menu includes east coast kippers with parsley butter, Macsween's haggis with a fried duck's egg,

glorious scrambled eggs and smoked salmon, smoked haddock kedgeree and

the inevitable magnificent full English. If you prefer something lighter there's porridge with berry compote or maple syrup, crushed avocado, tomato and chilli on granary toast, buckwheat crepe with coconut yogurt, or quinoa and pumpkin seed granola, plus croissants and pastries galore.

Not the cheapest place to start your day (full English £17), but certainly one of the most dramatic.

Plum & Spilt Milk, Great Northern Hotel, Pancras Rd, N1C 4TB (020-3388 0818, http:// plumandspiltmilk.com; King's Cross St Pancras tube/rail; breakfast Mon-Fri from 7am, weekends from 8am).

The Providores & Tapa Room

Run by Kiwi duo Peter Gordon (chef) and Michael McGrath (manager), the Providores & Tapa Room offers some of the most exciting and innovative fusion cuisine in London. On the ground floor is the laid-back Tapa Room (the name comes from the Pacific Rarotongan tapa cloth on the wall) –

an all-day café/wine bar – while upstairs is the more formal Providores dining room. The Tapa Room serves breakfast on weekdays and weekend brunch, while the Providores serves the same weekend brunch accompanied by a stunning dessert menu.

Both feature a wide choice of hot dishes showcasing ingredients from around the world, a selection of fry-ups and a delicious range of non-alcoholic cocktails such as a Virgin Mojito (lime, mint and lemonade). Stand-out dishes include Turkish eggs – inspired by a dish at Changa restaurant in Istanbul – which marries poached eggs with whipped yoghurt, hot chilli butter and sourdough toast. Then there's sweetcorn and blueberry fritters, with avocado, pomegranate and rocket salad; grilled sardines and roast tomato bruschetta; and roast Stornoway black pudding with baked apple and slow-roasted tomatoes. Desserts include the tongue-boggling treacle-cured bacon ice cream with olive meringues, banana salted caramel and yoghurt maple cream. Sublime!

You can book for brunch at Providores, but be prepared to queue for the Tapa Room.

The Providores & Tapa Room, 109 Marylebone High St, W1U 4RX (020-7935 6175; http:// theprovidores.co.uk; Baker St/Bond St tube; breakfast, Tapa Room Mon-Fri 9-11.30am; brunch, Tapa Room weekends 9am-3pm, Providores weekends 10am-2.45pm).

Raoul's

A trendy and stylish setting and a friendly and relaxed atmosphere, Raoul's flagship restaurant in Maida Vale has been a popular venue for breakfast or brunch for 30 years (there are also other branches in Hammersmith and Notting Hill). Weather permitting, try to nab one of the pavement tables with their big umbrellas.

The menu offers the usual breakfast dishes such as the ubiquitous full English, eggs on toast with bacon, sausages or smoked salmon, eggs Benedict or Florentine, poached smoked haddock or grilled kippers, *shakshuka* (spicy poached eggs), potato cakes and French toast with maple syrup or bacon. A speciality is one of Raoul's frittatas: try the chorizo, spring onion and parmesan. It's all served until noon, so you can take your time.

Raoul's, 13 Clifton Rd, London W9 1SZ (020-7289 7313; www.raoulsgourmet.com; Warwick Ave tube; breakfast/brunch, Mon-Fri 8.30am-noon, weekends 8.30am-6pm).

Roast

Opened in 2005 by restaurateur Iqbal Wahhab, award-winning Roast is located in the iconic Floral Hall at Borough Market (it once stood in Covent Garden but was moved and reconstucted here in 2004). Set over two levels, the spectacular elevated restaurant is a peaceful haven offering views of the Shard, St Paul's and the market below.

Roast's superb breakfast menu offers a choice of set menus including the Bubbly Breakfast (smoked trout, scrambled eggs and champagne), the Full Borough (English), the Full Scottish (with haggis, Lorne sausage and tattie scones) and the Veggie Borough. Other highlights include omelettes, dropped scones, Orkney kippers, smoked haddock, eggs Benedict or Royale, granola/muesli with prunes and yoghurt, and porridge with cream. Magic!

Roast, The Floral Hall, Stoney St, SE1 1TL (020-3006 6111; www.roast-restaurant.com; London Br tube; breakfast, Mon-Fri 7-11am, Sat 8-11.30am).

Sunday

By critical consensus, Sunday offers one of the best breakfast/brunch menus in North London (or even the world?). Certainly, there's no better place to spend a lazy Sunday (or any other day) than at this aptly-named café-restaurant, tastefully designed and located in a quiet residential street in Barnsbury and with a lovely garden, away from the hustle and bustle of Islington central.

Everything on the enticing all-day menu is scrumptious. Healthy types can tuck into granola with fruit and Greek yoghurt or quinoa, almond milk and maple syrup, while those in need of a hangover fix can get stuck into superb buttermilk pancakes with blueberries and bacon; brioche French toast with vanilla crème fraîche, banana and salted caramel; corn fritters with smoked salmon and avocado; or *huevos rotos* (broken eggs) with chorizo, potatoes, pepper, avocado and toast. Needless to say, Sunday serves a cracking full English, plus fantastic pastries, croissants and cakes (including gluten-free options), superb coffee, tea and juices.

For brunch there's more deliciousness, including creative salads (cured duck and goats curd, watermelon and feta, Parma ham and mozzarella), pasta dishes, beef carpaccio, confit duck leg, soft shell crab, risottos, scallops, and much, much more. You cannot book for brunch; just arrive early and expect to queue. Efficient, friendly service, fantastic food, relaxing atmosphere – Sunday scores a perfect 10!

Sunday, 169 Hemingford Rd, N1 1DA (020-7607 3868; Caledonian Rd & Barnsbury rail/ Caledonian Rd tube; breakfast, Tue-Fri from 8.30am; brunch, weekends from 10am, closed Mon).

Tom's Kitchen

Opened in 2006 by Michelin-starred chef Tom Aikens, Tom's Kitchen in Chelsea offers stonking weekday breakfasts and weekend brunches. Occupying a townhouse, site of the former pub *The Blenheim*, the modern British brasserie serves comfort-food favourites in a relaxed environment. The trailblazing décor – white tiles, marble counters, chunky wooden furniture, industrial-style lighting and open kitchen – was way ahead of its time and still looks bang on trend.

Tom's Kitchen uses the very best seasonal, local and ethically sourced ingredients, and serves fantastic fry-ups and excellent egg dishes. The menu caters to all breakfasters, from early birds to late risers, offering everything from croissants, granola and porridge to pancakes and waffles (with a dollop of cinnamon cream, caramelised apples and maple syrup), to mushrooms, avocado or black pudding on toast.

For those with a bigger appetite there's ham hock and mustard hash browns with poached egg and mustard sauce, maple cured gammon and eggs, smoked haddock kedgeree and a superb full English. The weekend brunch menu adds steak into the mix, plus the restaurant's range of mains and desserts. There's great coffee, fresh juices, milk shakes and the obligatory Bloody Mary.

Not the cheapest breakfast/brunch in town, but one of the very best.

Tom's Kitchen, 27 Cale St, SW3 3QP (020-7349 0202; www.tomskitchen.co.uk/chelsea; S Kensington tube; breakfast, Mon-Fri 8-11.30am, brunch, weekends 10am-3.30pm).

INDEX OF ENTRIES BY AREA

East

North

INDEX

About Survival Books

Survival Books was established in 1987 and by the mid-1990s was the leading publisher of books for expats and migrants planning to live, work, buy property and retire abroad. In 2000, we published the first of our London books, *Living and Working in London*, and since then we have added around 15 further London titles, including *London's Hidden Secrets* and *London's Secret Walks*, and we now specialise in alternative London guidebooks for both residents and visitors.

Our philosophy has always been to go the extra mile and provide the most accurate, comprehensive and up-to-date information available – our titles routinely contain much more information than similar books – and they are updated more frequently. All our London guidebooks are printed in colour and contain original illustrations, photographs and (where applicable) maps. Survival Books are designed to be easy – and interesting – to read, and invariably contain a comprehensive list of contents and/or index, so they are easy to navigate.

Our books are written by experts in their fields using their many years of first-hand experience and love of the city to unveil its secrets and give readers the inside info garnered over decades of living and working in London. They provide invaluable insights into local attractions and places that are off the beaten tourist track – information that cannot easily be obtained from official publications and is more comprehensive and reliable than that provided by the majority of official and unofficial websites.

See our websites for our latest titles: www.londons-secrets.com and www.survivalbooks.net

London's Secrets:
PEACEFUL PLACES

ISBN: 978-1-907339-45-5, 256 pages, hardback, £11.95

David Hampshire

London is one of the world's most exciting cities, but it's also one of the noisiest; a bustling, chaotic, frenetic, over-crowded, manic metropolis of over 8 million people, where it can be difficult to find somewhere to grab a little peace and quiet. Nevertheless, if you know where to look London has a wealth of peaceful places: places to relax, chill out, contemplate, meditate, sit, reflect, browse, read, chat, nap, walk, think, study or even work (if you must) – where the city's volume is muted or even switched off completely.

LONDON FOR FOODIES, GOURMETS & GLUTTONS

ISBN: 978-1-909282-76-6, 288 pages, hardback, £11.95

David Hampshire & Graeme Chesters

Much more than simply a directory of cafés, markets, restaurants and food shops, *London for Foodies, Gourmets & Gluttons* features many of the city's best artisan producers and purveyors, plus a wealth of classes where you can learn how to prepare and cook food like the experts, appreciate fine wines and brew coffee like a barista. And when you're too tired to cook or just want to treat yourself, we'll show you great places where you can enjoy everything from tea and cake to a tasty street snack; a pie and a pint to a glass of wine and tapas; and a quick working lunch to a full-blown gastronomic extravaganza.

see www.survivalbooks.net

London's Best-Kept Secrets

ISBN: 978-1-909282-74-2, 320 pages
£10.95, David Hampshire

London Best-Kept Secrets brings together our favourite places – the 'greatest hits' – from our London's Secrets series of books. We take you off the beaten tourist path to seek out the more unusual ('hidden') places that often fail to register on the radar of both visitors and residents alike. Nimbly sidestepping the chaos and queues of London's tourist-clogged attractions, we visit its quirkier, lesser-known, but no less fascinating, side. *London Best-Kept Secrets* takes in some of the city's loveliest hidden gardens and parks, absorbing and poignant museums, great art and architecture, beautiful ancient buildings, magnificent Victorian cemeteries, historic pubs, fascinating markets and much more.

London's Hidden Corners, Lanes & Squares

ISBN: 978-1-909282-69-8, 192 pages
£9.95, Graeme Chesters

The inspiration for this book was the advice of writer and lexicographer Dr Samuel Johnson (1709-1784), who was something of an expert on London, to his friend and biographer James Boswell on the occasion of his trip to London in the 18th century, to 'survey its innumerable little lane and courts'. In the 21st century these are less numerous than in Dr Johnson's time, so we've expanded his brief to include alleys, squares and yards, along with a number of mews, roads, streets and gardens.

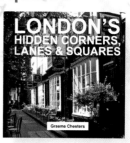

A Year in London: Two Things to Do Every Day of the Year

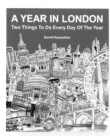

ISBN: 978-1-909282-68-1, 256 pages
£11.95, David Hampshire

London offers a wealth of things to do, from exuberant festivals and exciting sports events to a plethora of fascinating museums and stunning galleries, from luxury and oddball shops to first-class restaurants and historic pubs, beautiful parks and gardens to pulsating nightlife and clubs. Whatever your interests and tastes, you'll find an abundance of things to enjoy – with a copy of this book you'll never be at a loss for something to do in one of the world's greatest cities.

see www.londons-secrets.com

LONDON'S HIDDEN SECRETS
ISBN: 978-1-907339-40-0
£10.95, 320 pages
Graeme Chesters

A guide to London's hidden and lesser-known sights that aren't found in standard guidebooks. Step beyond the chaos, clichés and queues of London's tourist-clogged attractions to its quirkier side.

Discover its loveliest ancient buildings, secret gardens, strangest museums, most atmospheric pubs, cutting-edge art and design, and much more: some 140 destinations in all corners of the city.

LONDON'S HIDDEN SECRETS VOL. 2
ISBN: 978-1-907339-79-0
£10.95, 320 pages
Graeme Chesters & David Hampshire

Hot on the heels of London's Hidden Secrets comes another volume of the city's largely undiscovered sights, many of which we were unable to include in the original book. In fact, the more research we did the more treasures we found, until eventually a second volume was inevitable.

Written by two experienced London writers, LHS 2 is for both those who already know the metropolis and newcomers wishing to learn more about its hidden and unusual charms.

LONDON'S SECRET PLACES
ISBN: 978-1-907339-92-9
£10.95, 320 pages
Graeme Chesters & David Hampshire

London is one of the world's leading tourist destinations with a wealth of world-class attractions. These are covered in numerous excellent tourist guides and online, and need no introduction here.

Not so well known are London's numerous smaller attractions, most of which are neglected by the throngs who descend upon the tourist-clogged major sights. What London's Secret Places does is seek out the city's lesser-known, but no less worthy, 'hidden' attractions.

LONDON'S SECRET WALKS
ISBN: 978-1-907339-51-6
£11.95, 320 pages
Graeme Chesters

London is a great city for walking – whether for pleasure, exercise or simply to get from A to B. Despite the city's extensive public transport system, walking is often the quickest (and most enjoyable) way to get around – at least in the centre – and it's also free and healthy!

Many attractions are off the beaten track, away from the major thoroughfares and public transport hubs. This favours walking as the best way to explore them, as does the fact that London is a visually interesting city with a wealth of stimulating sights in every 'nook and cranny'.

also available as eBooks

LONDON'S SECRETS: BIZARRE & CURIOUS

ISBN: 978-1-909282-58-2

£11.95, 320 pages

Graeme Chesters

ndon is a city with over 2,000
ars of history, during which
has accumulated a wealth of
d and strange sights. This
ok seeks out the city's most
zarre and curious attractions
d tells the often fascinating
ry behind them, from the
ghgate vampire to the arrest
a dead man, a legal brothel
d a former Texas embassy
Roman bikini bottoms and
etic manhole covers, from
ndon's hanging gardens to
estaurant where you dine in
e dark.

Bizarre & Curious is sure to
ep you amused and fascinated
hours.

LONDON'S SECRETS: MUSEUMS & GALLERIES

ISBN: 978-1-907339-96-7

£10.95, 320 pages

Robbi Atilgan & David Hampshire

London is a treasure trove for
museum fans and art lovers and
one of the world's great art and
cultural centres. The art scene is
a lot like the city itself – diverse,
vast, vibrant and in a constant
state of flux – a cornucopia of
traditional and cutting-edge,
majestic and mundane, world-
class and run-of-the-mill, bizarre
and brilliant.

So, whether you're an art lover,
culture vulture, history buff or just
looking for something to entertain
the family during the school
holidays, you're bound to find
inspiration in London.

LONDON'S SECRETS: PARKS & GARDENS

ISBN: 978-1-907339-95-0

£10.95, 320 pages

Robbi Atilgan & David Hampshire

London is one of the world's
greenest capital cities, with a
wealth of places where you
can relax and recharge your
batteries.

Britain is renowned for its
parks and gardens, and nowhere
has such beautiful and varied
green spaces as London:
magnificent royal parks, historic
garden cemeteries, majestic
ancient forests and woodlands,
breathtaking formal country
parks, expansive commons,
charming small gardens, beautiful
garden squares and enchanting
'secret' gardens.

LONDON'S SECRETS: PUBS & BARS

ISBN: 978-1-907339-93-6

£10.95, 320 pages

Graeme Chesters

British pubs and bars are world
famous for their bonhomie,
great atmosphere, good food
and fine ales.

Nowhere is this more so than
in London, which has a plethora
of watering holes of all shapes
and sizes: classic historic boozers
and trendy style bars; traditional
riverside inns and luxurious
cocktail bars; enticing wine bars
and brew pubs; mouth-watering
gastro pubs and brasseries;
welcoming gay bars and raucous
music venues. This book
highlights over 250 of the best.

see www.londons-secrets.com

London Sketchbook

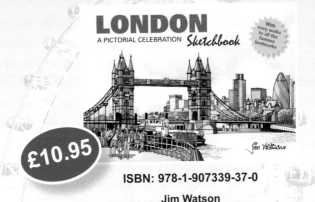

£10.95

ISBN: 978-1-907339-37-0

Jim Watson

A celebration of one of the world's great cities, *London Sketchbook* is a hardback packed with over 200 evocative watercolour illustrations of the author's favourite landmarks and sights. The illustrations are accompanied by historical footnotes, maps, walks, quirky facts and a gazetteer.

Also in this series:

Cornwall Sketchbook (ISBN: 9781909282780, £10.95)
Cotswold Sketchbook (ISBN: 9781907339108, £9.95)
Devon Sketchbook (ISBN: 9781909282704, £10.95)
Lake District Sketchbook (ISBN: 9781909282605, £10.95)
Yorkshire Sketchbook (ISBN: 9781909282773, £10.95)

see www.survivalbooks.net